Dubai Travel Guide 2024

Journey Through Time, Your Essential 2024 Travel Companion

Melody J. Clark

1

TABLE OF CONTENTS

FACTS ABOUT DURBAN 6

FAQS ABOUT DURBAN 8

INTRODUCTION TO DURBAN 12

WELCOME TO DURBAN 12
HISTORY AND CULTURE 14
GETTING AROUND 17

ESSENTIAL TRAVEL INFORMATION 20

VISA REQUIREMENTS 20
CURRENCY AND EXCHANGE 24
HEALTH AND SAFETY TIPS 27

TRANSPORTATION GUIDE 30

PUBLIC TRANSPORTATION 30
CAR RENTALS 33
TAXI SERVICES 36

ACCOMMODATION OPTIONS 40

LUXURY HOTELS 40
BUDGET HOSTELS 42
BED AND BREAKFASTS 45

TOP ATTRACTIONS IN DURBAN 48

BEACHES AND WATERFRONTS 48

MUSEUMS AND ART GALLERIES 51

WILDLIFE PARKS AND RESERVES 54

OUTDOOR ADVENTURES 58

SURFING AND WATERSPORTS 58

HIKING TRAILS 61

SAFARI TOURS 63

CULINARY DELIGHTS 66

TRADITIONAL SOUTH AFRICAN CUISINE 66

FUSION RESTAURANTS 69

STREET FOOD HOTSPOTS 72

NIGHTLIFE AND ENTERTAINMENT 76

BARS AND CLUBS 76

LIVE MUSIC VENUES 79

THEATRES AND CINEMAS 82

SHOPPING IN DURBAN 86

MARKETS AND BAZAARS 86

SHOPPING MALLS 89

LOCAL CRAFTS AND SOUVENIRS 92

DAY TRIPS AND EXCURSIONS 96

DURBAN TO PIETERMARITZBURG 96

DOLPHIN COAST TOUR   98
VALLEY OF A THOUSAND HILLS   100

EVENTS AND FESTIVALS   102

DURBAN JULY   102
CULTURAL FESTIVALS   104
FOOD AND WINE EVENTS   107

LANGUAGE AND CULTURE   110

ZULU LANGUAGE BASICS   110
CULTURAL ETIQUETTE   113
TRADITIONAL CUSTOMS   116

HEALTH AND WELLNESS   120

SPA RETREATS   120
YOGA STUDIOS   123

PHOTOGRAPHY GUIDE   126

BEST PHOTOGRAPHY SPOTS   126
TIPS FOR CAPTURING DURBAN'S ESSENCE   130

PLANNING YOUR TRIP   134

ITINERARY SUGGESTIONS   134
PACKING TIPS   137

CONCLUSION   140

MAP OF DURBAN

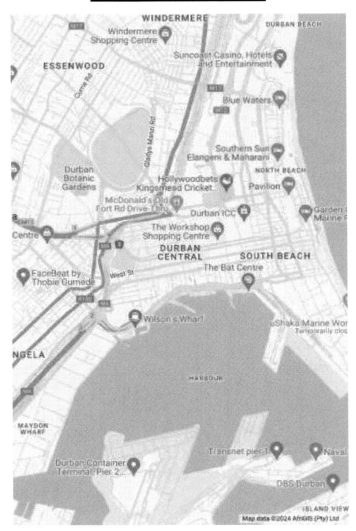

FACTS ABOUT DURBAN

1. Durban is the third largest city in South Africa, behind Johannesburg and Cape Town.

2. It is the largest city in KwaZulu-Natal province, South Africa.

3. Durban has a subtropical climate with warm, humid summers and moderate winters, making it a popular year-round vacation.

4. The Golden Mile, a 6 km (almost 4 mile) section of the Indian Ocean coastline, is well-known for its stunning beaches.

Durban's diverse culture, including a large Indian community, has affected the city's cuisine, architecture, and cultural customs.

6. Durban's Moses Mabhida Stadium hosted the 2010 FIFA World Cup.

7. Durban is Africa's largest port, which handles significant cargo volumes and serves as an important commerce gateway in the area.

8. The city's skyline is dominated by uShaka Marine World, one of the world's largest aquariums with diverse marine life and exhilarating water attractions.

9. Durban is known as "Surf City" for its ideal surfing conditions and for holding international championships.

10. The Durban Botanic Gardens, established in 1849, is Africa's oldest botanical garden with a diverse variety of indigenous and foreign species.

Inanda, a Durban suburb, is historically significant as the location where Mahatma Gandhi formed his passive resistance concept, Satyagraha, while in South Africa.

12. Visitors to Durban may witness traditional Zulu dancing, music, and festivities.

13. The city's diversified culinary sector offers a variety of cuisines, including hot Indian curries and delicious seafood meals.

14. Durban's thriving street markets, including Victoria Street Market and Warwick Junction Market, provide a variety of commodities, spices, and local crafts.

Durban's rich history, cultural variety, and gorgeous natural surroundings make it a popular tourist destination in South Africa, offering sun, sea, and unique experiences.

FAQs ABOUT DURBAN

What is Durban known for?

Durban is well-known for its gorgeous beaches, rich cultural variety, and busy street markets.

What's the weather like in Durban?

Durban's climate is subtropical, with warm, humid summers and moderate, dry winters. Temperatures normally vary from 20°C to 30°C (68°F to 86°F) in the summer and 10°C to 20°C (50°F to 68°F) in winter.

Which are the nicest beaches in Durban?

Umhlanga Rocks Beach, North Beach, and South Beach on the Golden Mile are among Durban's top beaches.

How can I navigate Durban with public transportation?

Durban has a reliable public transit system that comprises buses, minibusses, and Metrorail's commuter rail network. Taxis and ride-hailing services are also widely accessible.

What are the top attractions in Durban?

The top attractions in Durban include uShaka Marine World, Moses Mabhida Stadium, Durban Botanic Gardens, and Victoria Street Market.

What are some of Durban's family-friendly activities?

Family-friendly activities in Durban include visiting uShaka Marine World, experiencing Mitchell Park Zoo, and spending the day at Suncoast Casino and Entertainment World.

Where are the greatest seafood restaurants in Durban?

Some of Durban's top seafood restaurants are found along the seaside promenade and in the Victoria Street Market area.

What cultural experiences may I enjoy in Durban?

Visitors visiting Durban may learn about Zulu culture at the Shakaland Cultural Village, see the Indian Quarter, and visit historical places such as the Mahatma Gandhi Settlement.

Are there any wildlife parks or reserves nearby Durban?

Yes, Hluhluwe-iMfolozi Park and iSimangaliso Wetland Park are both within driving distance of Durban and provide animal watching and safari trips.

What are the finest spots to stay in Durban?

Umhlanga, Durban North, and the seaside region along the Golden Mile are popular Durban accommodation options.

How secure is Durban for tourists?

Like any large metropolis, it is critical to stay watchful, especially in specific locations. However, Durban is typically safe for travelers who exercise caution and use common sense safety precautions.

Which languages are spoken in Durban?

English is the most commonly spoken language in Durban, followed by Zulu. Due to the city's varied population, you may hear Afrikaans and other Indian languages spoken.

Are there any renowned events or festivals in Durban?

Yes, Durban holds several events and festivals throughout the year, including the Durban July Horse Race, the Durban International Film Festival, and the Essence Festival Durban.

What outdoor activities may I do in Durban?

Durban and its neighboring environs offer opportunities for outdoor enthusiasts to surf, swim, dive, hike, and mountain bike.

What is the history of Durban?

Durban has a rich history extending back to the early nineteenth century when it was established as a British outpost. It had an important role in South Africa's colonial and apartheid history, and it has since become a symbol of cultural variety and perseverance.

How can I learn to surf in Durban?

Several surf schools along the Golden Mile provide training for both beginners and expert surfers, offering an ideal chance to catch some waves in Durban's warm seas.

What shopping options are there in Durban?

Durban has a diversified shopping experience, with modern malls like Gateway Theatre of Shopping and historic marketplaces like Victoria Street Market selling everything from souvenirs to spices.

Are there any day trips or excursions that I can do from Durban?

Yes, you may take day trips from Durban to destinations like the Valley of a Thousand Hills, the Drakensberg Mountains, and the Midlands Meander, all of which offer distinct landscapes and cultural experiences.

What are the greatest vantage locations for panoramic views of Durban?

The Moses Mabhida Stadium provides a SkyCar trip to the summit for breathtaking views of the city and coastline. The Durban Botanic Gardens and Umhlanga Lighthouse provide wonderful observation locations.

What should I take for my vacation to Durban?

A vacation to Durban requires lightweight clothing, sunscreen, a hat, sunglasses, a swimsuit, and comfortable walking shoes. It is also suggested to bring bug repellent and a reusable water bottle.

INTRODUCTION TO DURBAN

Welcome To Durban

We are delighted to send our warmest wishes as you begin your trip to experience the exciting city of Durban. As you enter this seaside jewel, let us be your trusted guide, improving your experience and ensuring that every moment spent here leaves an everlasting stamp on your memories.

Nestled along the golden coastline of the Indian Ocean, Durban entices a symphony of sights, sounds, and smells ready to be discovered. From the sun-kissed beaches of the famed Golden Mile to the busy streets brimming with activity, every part of this city is a treasure mine of experiences just waiting to be discovered.

As a fellow traveler who has been through the streets of Durban several times, I can vouch for the wonder that awaits you. From the time you arrive, you'll be immersed in the unique tapestry of cultures that characterize this city, from the exuberant rhythms of Zulu music to the enticing fragrances of Indian spices floating through the air. But Durban is more than simply a place; it's a feeling, a sense of belonging that washes over you like the soothing waves of the sea. It's in the joy of children playing on the beach, the pleasant grins of residents ready to share their experiences, and the sense of community that cuts over language boundaries. As you begin your vacation, remember to cherish each minute and immerse yourself in the rhythm of Durban life. Whether you're eating delicious seafood at a coastal café, browsing the vivid booths of a local market, or simply watching the sunset paint the sky in orange and gold, make every encounter a celebration of the beauty that surrounds you.

So, dear tourist, when you go out to discover the delights of Durban, remember that you are more than a visitor; you are a valued guest, welcomed with open arms and limitless possibilities. May your stay here be full of joy, exploration, and experiences that will last a lifetime.

Welcome to Durban, where each moment is an adventure waiting to happen.

History And Culture

Durban, located on South Africa's eastern coast, is a witness to the convergence of many cultures and a rich history that has defined its character over generations. From its humble origins as an indigenous village to its growth as a bustling city, Durban's history is a riveting trip through time, full of victories, hardships, and perseverance.

> Early Settlements and Indigenous Peoples.

Durban's history dates back thousands of years, when the territory was inhabited by indigenous cultures, including the Khoisan and Nguni peoples. These early immigrants lived off the land, hunting, collecting, and forming tiny villages along the shore and interior.

> European Exploration and Colonization

The entrance of European explorers in the fifteenth century was a watershed point in Durban's history. Portuguese navigators were among the first to map the coastline, followed by Dutch and British businessmen looking to develop trade routes and colonies in the area. Lieutenant F. G. Farewell, a British colonial governor, founded a trading post on what is now known as Durban in 1824, laying the framework for the city's future growth. The colony, once known as Port Natal, was an important trading hub for European merchants and indigenous peoples.

> The arrival of Indian and colonial influences

Durban's cultural environment changed dramatically in the mid-nineteenth century with the introduction of Indian indentured laborers brought to work on sugar estates. This flood of Indian migrants, together with British colonial authorities and immigrants, enriched the city's cultural variety and provided the groundwork for its multicultural character.

The Indian population had a significant impact on Durban's culture, bringing features of Indian food, music, and religious rituals that are still prevalent today. The lively marketplaces, scented spice shops, and magnificent temples dotting the metropolis reflect the impact of Indian culture.

> The Struggle Against Apartheid and the Road to Democracy

Durban saw enormous social and political turmoil during the twentieth century as South Africa dealt with the harsh apartheid system. Durban, like many other cities in the country, became a battleground for the fight against racial segregation and discrimination. The Durban Strikes of 1973, led by Indian workers opposing unfair labor practices, and the Soweto Uprising of 1976, triggered by the adoption of Afrikaans as a language of instruction in schools, were watershed moments in Durban's anti-apartheid movement. Durban was an important city in the democratic movement, providing a gathering point for political leaders, activists, and regular residents who were all fighting for freedom and equality. The city saw momentous events such as Nelson Mandela's release from jail in 1990 and the first democratic elections in 1994, which signaled the end of apartheid and the start of a new era in South Africa.

> Celebrate Diversity and Cultural Heritage

Today, Durban is a symbol of multiculturalism and variety, embracing a complex tapestry of cultures and customs. The city's cultural environment is a dynamic mix of Zulu, Indian, British, and other influences, as seen in its food, architecture, festivals, and traditions.

From the vibrant festivals of Diwali and Eid to the rhythmic rhythms of Zulu dance and music, Durban's cultural calendar is jam-packed with events that highlight the city's distinct heritage. Visitors may visit historic places, including the Mahatma Gandhi Settlement, the KwaMuhle Museum, and the Durban Botanic Gardens, which provide insights into Durban's history and present.

History and culture in Durban are not limited to museums or monuments; they are woven into the fabric of everyday life, defining the city's character and enhancing the lives of individuals who live there. As Durban evolves and faces new challenges, its history and culture will continue to be a source of pride and inspiration for future generations.

Getting Around

Navigating Durban's crowded thoroughfares and different neighborhoods is an experience in and of itself. From public transit to vehicle rentals and more, here's everything you need to know to travel around Durban with comfort and confidence.

> ➤ Public Transportation

Durban has a robust public transit system that serves both locals and visitors alike. The Durban People Mover, a fleet of contemporary buses that travels essential routes around the city center and beachside districts, serves as the city's transportation network's backbone. The People Mover offers a simple and economical method to visit Durban's best attractions, retail malls, and hotels.

In addition to the People Mover, Durban has a network of minibusses, known as taxis, that run on predetermined routes and offer an essential link to distant districts and slums. Taxis provide flexibility and accessibility, although they can be congested and unreliable during rush hours. Metrorail provides commuter train services that connect Durban with adjacent cities and suburbs for individuals who want to go outside of the city. While rail travel is slower than other modes of transportation, it allows you to see the beautiful scenery of KwaZulu-Natal.

> ➤ Car Rentals

Renting a car is a popular choice for those looking for flexibility and convenience when touring Durban and its neighboring areas. Several reliable automobile rental businesses operate in the area, offering a diverse selection of vehicles to fit any budget or inclination.

Driving about Durban allows you to explore at your speed, go off the main road, and uncover hidden treasures that may not be accessible by public transit. However, it is critical to become acquainted with local traffic rules and road conditions, as well as practice caution, especially during high-traffic hours.

> ➢ Taxi Services

In addition to minibusses, Durban has metered taxis and ride-hailing services like Uber and Bolt, which provide passengers with efficient door-to-door transit choices. Metered taxis can be hailed on the street or reserved in advance, whilst ride-hailing services provide the ease of reserving journeys using a smartphone app. Whether you're traveling to the airport, experiencing the city's nightlife, or simply need a ride to your hotel, taxi services provide a simple and dependable method to move around Durban, especially for short distances or late-night travel.

> ➢ Biking and Walking

Biking and walking are good modes of transportation for eco-conscious travelers or those who want to explore Durban's neighborhoods at their leisure. The city has a network of designated bike lanes and picturesque waterfront promenades, making it simple to ride from one destination to the next. Exploring Durban by foot allows you to fully immerse yourself in the city's sights, sounds, and fragrances, from the busy marketplaces of Warwick Junction to the peaceful green areas of the Durban Botanic Gardens. Walking also has the bonus of allowing you to find hidden jewels and local sites that you may otherwise miss.

> ➢ Accessibility & Special Services

Durban is dedicated to offering accessible transportation choices for people with disabilities, including wheelchair-accessible buses and taxis outfitted with ramps and lifts. Furthermore, many attractions, retail malls, and public areas in Durban are wheelchair accessible, ensuring that all tourists may fully enjoy the city's offerings. Durban's tourism information centers and hotels offer advice and help to visitors who require particular assistance or accommodations, guaranteeing a seamless and delightful experience for everybody.

To summarize, exploring Durban is an interesting and gratifying experience, with a variety of transportation alternatives to fit every traveler's interests and tastes. Whether you use public transit, rent a vehicle, call a cab, or simply stroll through the city streets, Durban welcomes you on a voyage of discovery and adventure unlike any other.

ESSENTIAL TRAVEL INFORMATION

Visa Requirements

Before you travel to the exciting city of Durban, you must first grasp the visa requirements for your stay. Whether you're visiting Durban for tourism, business, or another reason, here's everything you need to know to have a seamless and hassle-free arrival.

➢ Tourist visas

For many tourists visiting Durban, acquiring a tourist visa is a simple process. Citizens of some countries, including the United States, Canada, the European Union, Australia, and New Zealand, can enter South Africa without a visa for stays of up to 90 days. This visa exemption allows people to visit Durban and other South African sites for leisure, sightseeing, and recreational activities without requiring a visa. However, it is essential to examine the precise visa requirements for your place of citizenship, as visa restrictions might differ based on your nationality. Some nations may require tourists to get a tourist visa in advance or upon arrival in South Africa. Additionally, tourists should check that their passport is valid for at least six months after their scheduled departure date from South Africa.

➢ Business visas

A business visa may be required for visitors to Durban who are attending meetings, conferences, or trade events. Business visas are often granted to those who want to conduct business activity or represent their firm while in

South Africa. To apply for a business visa, visitors may need to supply paperwork such as a letter of invitation from a South African host firm, proof of adequate finances to cover their stay, and itinerary and hotel details. Consult the nearest South African embassy or consulate for precise visa requirements and application procedures.

> Work visas

Individuals wishing to work or engage in employment activities in Durban must get a work visa. Work visas are granted to foreign nationals who have found work with a South African employer and satisfy the standards established by the South African Department of Home Affairs. To apply for a work visa, candidates may need to produce paperwork such as a job offer letter, proof of credentials or experience, and proof of conformity with South African immigration regulations. Work visa applications must be sent to the South African Department of Home Affairs or the nearest South African embassy or consulate in the applicant's place of residence.

> Student visas

Obtaining a student visa is an important step in the enrollment process for overseas students who want to study at Durban universities or educational institutions. Student visas are granted to foreign citizens who have been accepted into a recognized academic program in South Africa and fulfill the visa conditions. To apply for a student visa, applicants may be required to produce paperwork such as a letter of admission from a South African educational institution, proof of adequate means to cover tuition and living expenses, and proof of medical insurance. Student visa applications must be sent to the South African Department of Home Affairs or the nearest

South African embassy or consulate in the applicant's place of residence.

> Transit visas

A transit visa may be necessary for passengers passing through South Africa on their way to their final destination, depending on the length of their stopover and their nationality. Transit visas are often provided to those who are traveling through South Africa and do not intend to leave the airport or stay for a prolonged amount of time.

To apply for a transit visa, passengers may need to give proof of onward travel, a valid visa for their ultimate destination, and information on their itinerary and lodging arrangements. Transit visa applications must be filed to the South African Department of Home Affairs or the nearest South African embassy or consulate in the traveler's home country.

> Important Considerations:

When planning your trip to Durban, make sure you understand the precise visa requirements that relate to your position and nationality. Visa requirements may differ based on the purpose of your travel, the duration of your stay, and your place of citizenship.

To guarantee a seamless and hassle-free arrival in Durban, passengers should:

Check the visa requirements for South Africa well ahead of their scheduled travel.

Gather all of the papers and information required for the visa application procedure.

Submit visa applications on time and following any instructions issued by immigration officials.

Ensure that their passport is valid for at least six months after the scheduled departure date from South Africa.

While in South Africa, visitors must follow all immigration rules and regulations, as well as any visa limitations. Understanding and following the visa requirements for Durban allows tourists to have a smooth and pleasurable trip seeing this bustling coastal city and all it has to offer. Whether you're here for vacation, business, or education, Durban greets you warmly and offers an amazing trip in one of South Africa's most active and culturally diverse cities.

Currency And Exchange

As you plan your trip to the exciting city of Durban, it is essential to understand the local currency and exchange alternatives to ensure a smooth and pleasurable stay. From currency denominations to exchange rates and banking options, here's everything you need to know about managing your money while visiting Durban's many attractions.

➢ Local Currency

South Africa's national currency is the South African Rand (ZAR), which is abbreviated as "R" or "ZAR." The Rand is divisible into 100 cents, and coins come in denominations of 1, 2, 5, 10, 20, and 50 cents, as well as 1, 2, and 5 Rand. Banknotes come in denominations of 10, 20, 50, 100, and 200 Rand.

➢ Currency Exchange

Currency exchange services are widely available in Durban, with banks, currency exchange bureaus, and hotels providing simple ways to convert foreign currencies into South African Rand. Furthermore, large airports, retail malls, and tourist destinations frequently feature specialized currency exchange kiosks where visitors may convert money at favorable rates.

When converting currencies, compare exchange rates and fees to ensure you receive the greatest value for your money. Some currency exchange services may charge commission fees or offer less favorable rates, so ask about any additional expenses before completing your transaction.

➢ ATMs and Banking Facilities

Durban has a well-developed financial system, with several ATMs and banking facilities located around the city. ATMs are widely available in shopping malls, hotels, and tourist destinations, providing easy access to cash withdrawals and other financial services.

Most ATMs in Durban accept major international credit and debit cards, such as Visa, MasterCard, American Express, and Diners Club. However, you must advise your bank of your vacation intentions and inquire about any international transaction fees or withdrawal limitations that may apply to your account. When using ATMs in Durban, be cautious and be aware of your surroundings to prevent being a victim of opportunistic crime. Choose ATMs in well-lit and crowded places, and cover your PIN when entering it to avoid potential skimming devices.

> Credit Cards & Payment Options

Credit cards are commonly accepted at Durban's hotels, restaurants, stores, and other facilities, especially in tourist and affluent neighborhoods. The most generally accepted credit card brands are Visa and Mastercard, while certain companies may take American Express and Diners Club.

Before using your credit card in Durban, notify your card issuer of your trip intentions to avoid any complications with card authorization or security. Additionally, be aware that certain companies may impose minimum purchase quantities or fees for credit card purchases, so it's always a good idea to have some cash on hand as a backup.

> Currency Tips and Considerations

Before visiting Durban, familiarize yourself with the current conversion rate between your local money and the South African rand. Carry a combination of cash and credit/debit cards for flexibility and convenience, especially when visiting remote locations or smaller businesses that may not take credit cards.

Keep track of your bank's contact information and card data in case of an emergency or problems with your accounts while abroad. Carry large quantities of cash with caution, and keep valuables secure to reduce the chance of theft or loss.

Understanding the local currency and exchange alternatives in Durban allows you to manage your funds properly and enjoy a worry-free time while seeing the diverse sights, sounds, and smells of this dynamic coastal city. Whether you're looking for souvenirs at a lively market, dining at a world-class restaurant, or going on an adventure along the gorgeous coastline, Durban welcomes you with open arms and offers an exciting trip full of cultural discoveries and memorable encounters.

Health And Safety Tips

As you go out to explore the dynamic city of Durban, it's critical to prioritize your health and safety to guarantee a memorable and worry-free trip. From staying hydrated in the subtropical environment to confidently navigating the city's different neighborhoods, here are some general health and safety advice to keep in mind throughout your trip.

➢ Stay hydrated and sun safe.

Durban's subtropical climate ensures pleasant temperatures and lots of sunshine all year round. To minimize dehydration and sunburn, drink lots of water throughout the day and use high-SPF sunscreen before going outside. Wearing a hat, sunglasses, and lightweight, breathable clothes can also help shield you from the sun's rays while visiting the city.

➢ Practice Safe Food and Water Hygiene.

When dining out in Durban, it is essential to maintain good food and drink hygiene to avoid foodborne diseases. Choose trustworthy restaurants and food sellers with clean, hygienic facilities, and avoid eating raw or undercooked meals, especially seafood. Additionally, drink bottled or filtered water to eliminate any pollutants, and wash and peel fruits and vegetables well before eating.

➢ Be aware of the potential health risks.

While Durban is usually regarded as a safe location for tourists, it is essential to be aware of any health hazards and take the appropriate steps to protect yourself. Mosquito-borne illnesses like malaria and dengue fever are uncommon in cities like Durban, but they can be dangerous in rural or coastal locations. Consider applying insect repellent, wearing long sleeves and pants, and sleeping under mosquito nets, especially if you're going to isolated places or during the rainy season.

> Stay informed and prepared.

Before flying to Durban, it is recommended that you remain up to date on any health warnings or travel alerts issued by local authorities or international health organizations. Familiarize yourself with the emergency contact information for local hospitals, clinics, and emergency services, and consider obtaining travel insurance to cover any unexpected medical bills or emergencies that arise during your trip.

> Practice personal safety measures.

As with any big city, it is important to take personal safety precautions to safeguard yourself and your property when visiting Durban. Avoid going alone in unfamiliar or poorly lit locations, especially at night, and exercise caution in popular tourist areas where pickpocketing and petty crime may occur. Keep valuables like passports, cash, and electronic gadgets safe and out of sight, and consider utilizing a money belt or concealed bag for extra precaution.

> Respect the local customs and cultural norms.

Respecting local customs and cultural standards is vital for having a happy and peaceful stay in Durban. When visiting religious places or engaging in cultural activities, be aware of clothing requirements and obtain permission before photographing persons or sacred locations. Show your admiration for the local culture by learning a few simple Zulu words or greeting residents with a cheerful "Sawubona" (hello) or "Ngikhona" (I am here).

Following these thorough health and safety precautions will allow you to have a safe, healthy, and rewarding time while experiencing the exciting city of Durban. Taking proactive actions to prioritize your well-being, from being hydrated and sun-safe to adopting personal safety precautions and respecting local customs, will ensure a pleasurable and worry-free vacation to this vibrant seaside resort.

TRANSPORTATION GUIDE

Public Transportation

The robust public transit system in Durban makes it easy and comfortable to navigate the city's colorful streets. From contemporary buses to commuter trains and informal minibusses, Durban provides a variety of transportation alternatives for visitors to explore the city and its surroundings. Here's all you need to know about public transit in Durban:

> Durban People Mover

The Durban People Mover is the city's primary mode of public transit, providing residents and visitors with quick and economical transportation. This contemporary bus service runs on specified routes across the city center and beachside districts, making stops at important attractions, shopping malls, and hotels. The Durban People Mover provides regular service and luxurious facilities like air conditioning and onboard Wi-Fi, making it a handy way to visit Durban's major locations.

> Commuter trains

Metrorail provides commuter train services that connect Durban with adjacent cities and suburbs for travelers who want to journey outside the city limits. These trains offer a cost-effective and efficient mode of transportation for both commuters and leisure travelers, with lines connecting Pietermaritzburg, Ballito, and Richards Bay. While train travel is slower than other modes of transportation, it allows you to enjoy the stunning landscapes of KwaZulu-Natal while also connecting with local communities along the route.

> Minibuses (taxi)

In addition to regular public transit, Durban has a network of minibusses, sometimes known as taxis, that travel on fixed routes around the city and neighboring areas. These minibusses connect remote neighborhoods and townships, providing passengers with flexibility and accessibility. While taxis can be congested and unreliable during rush hours, they are a handy and economical way to move around Durban, especially for short trips or places not served by other modes of public transit.

> Ride-hailing services

Ride-hailing services such as Uber and Bolt operate in Durban, enabling simple door-to-door transportation with the push of a button. These smartphone applications let passengers request trips from local drivers and watch their progress in real-time, providing a more convenient and dependable alternative to traditional taxis. Ride-hailing services are a popular alternative for tourists looking for flexibility and convenience during their stay in Durban since they provide low pricing and a variety of vehicle options.

> Accessibility

Durban is dedicated to offering accessible transportation choices for people with disabilities, including wheelchair-accessible buses and taxis outfitted with ramps and lifts. Furthermore, many public transportation stations and vehicles are intended to accommodate passengers with mobility issues, ensuring that everyone may benefit from Durban's public transportation system.

> Tips For Using Public Transportation

31

When utilizing public transit in Durban, keep the following things in mind to guarantee a seamless and pleasurable experience. Plan your itinerary and become acquainted with the timetables and itineraries of the Durban People Mover, Metrorail, and minibusses. Purchase your tickets or fares in advance, either online or at a recognized ticket office or machine. When using public transit, be mindful of your surroundings and keep valuables secure, especially in crowded or busy locations. Respect fellow passengers and follow any rules or regulations stated on public transit vehicles or terminals.

Using Durban's extensive public transit system, visitors may easily and conveniently tour the city and its surroundings, making the most of their time in this exciting seaside destination. Whether you're visiting for business or leisure, public transit is a simple and cost-effective way to explore everything Durban has to offer.

Car Rentals

In Durban, the entrance to South Africa's intriguing KwaZulu-Natal region, vehicle rentals allow visitors to explore the city and its surroundings at their leisure. With a profusion of reliable rental businesses and a variety of vehicle options to pick from, renting a car in Durban is a quick and hassle-free way to start your vacation. Here's what you should know about automobile rentals in Durban:

> ➤ Options and Availability.

Durban has a broad range of vehicle rental providers, ranging from major names to local operators, all competing to meet the demands of discriminating guests. Whether you're searching for a tiny sedan to cruise the city streets or a robust SUV to explore the countryside, you'll find a variety of cars to meet your needs and budget.

> ➤ Rental Locations

Car rental companies are easily accessible across Durban, with pick-up and drop-off locations at important transit hubs such as King Shaka International Airport, Durban Station, and major hotels and shopping malls. Many rental companies now offer one-way rentals, which allow you to pick up your vehicle at one place and return it at another, giving you more flexibility with your travel plans.

> ➤ Booking and Reservation

Booking a rental car in Durban is simple, with the option to reserve your vehicle online, via phone, or in person at a rental agency. Advance booking is encouraged, especially during high travel seasons or for specialist vehicles, to assure availability and the best pricing. Most rental firms require renters to be at least 21 years old and have a valid driver's license, however, age limitations and extra criteria may differ based on the rental company and vehicle type.

> ➤ Insurance and Coverage

When renting a car in Durban, it is essential to understand the insurance choices and coverage provided by the rental provider. Collision damage waiver (CDW) and theft protection are common features of basic insurance coverage, but extra choices like supplementary liability insurance (SLI) and personal accident insurance (PAI) may be offered for further peace of mind. Make sure to thoroughly read the terms and conditions of your rental agreement, and consider obtaining additional coverage if necessary.

> ➤ Driving in Durban.

Durban's streets and highways are generally easy to navigate, thanks to well-maintained roads and visible signage that direct cars to their destination. However, you should be aware of local traffic rules and regulations, such as speed limits, road signs, and driving etiquette. Keep in mind that in South Africa, driving is on the left side of the road, and seat belts are required for all vehicle occupants. Furthermore, use caution when driving at night, especially in rural regions where wildlife might pose a threat on the road.

> ➤ Exploring beyond Durban

One of the most significant benefits of renting a car in Durban is the ability to explore the different landscapes and attractions of KwaZulu-Natal at your own leisure.

From the breathtaking Drakensberg Mountains to the pristine beaches of the South Coast and the ancient battlefields of Zululand, there are plenty of locations to explore within a short drive from Durban. With a rented automobile, the opportunities for adventure are limitless. With accessible rental locations, low pricing, and a diverse range of vehicles to pick from, renting a car in Durban is the ideal option to maximize the potential of your trip experience.

Taxi Services

Taxi services in Durban are a handy and dependable means of transportation for both residents and visitors, giving door-to-door service and flexibility for travelers visiting the city and its surroundings. Here's all you need to know about taxi services in Durban, including metered taxis and ride-hailing services:

> Metered taxis

Metered taxis are widespread on Durban's streets, providing passengers with a controlled and metered fee structure. These cabs may be hailed on the street or reserved in advance via a taxi dispatch service or smartphone app. Metered taxis are widely available around the city and are a popular alternative for those looking for a simple and hassle-free mode of transportation.

> Ride-hailing services

In recent years, ride-hailing services like Uber and Bolt have grown in popularity in Durban, offering an alternative to traditional metered taxis. These smartphone applications enable customers to request trips from local drivers and follow their routes in real-time, providing convenience and flexibility to travelers. Ride-hailing services often provide upfront pricing and the opportunity to pay electronically through the app, making them an attractive choice for travelers who do not have cash on hand.

> Informal minibuses (Taxi)

In addition to professional taxi services, Durban is served by a network of informal minibusses, sometimes known as taxis, that travel on predetermined routes around the city and neighboring areas. These minibusses connect remote neighborhoods and townships, providing passengers with flexibility and accessibility. While informal taxis are not as strictly regulated as metered taxis, they are a popular and cost-effective choice for both locals and visitors.

> Airport Taxis

Taxis are easily accessible outside the arrivals area at King Shaka International Airport, providing quick transportation to places around Durban and beyond. Airport taxis operate on a set fare system, with charges defined by distance traveled and destination. Travelers should utilize only approved airport taxi services and check the fare with the driver before leaving.

> Tips For Using Taxi Services

When utilizing taxi services in Durban, keep the following recommendations in mind to guarantee a seamless and pleasurable experience:

Always utilize legal and reliable taxi services, whether you hail one on the street or order through a smartphone app.

Confirm the fare with the driver before beginning your journey, and be ready to pay in cash or online, depending on the payment options offered.

When traveling by cab, keep valuables such as passports, cash, and electronic gadgets secure and out of sight.

When traveling late at night or in unknown regions, use caution and heed your instincts if you feel uncomfortable or dangerous.

By following these suggestions and using trustworthy taxi services, visitors to Durban may have a pleasant and hassle-free transportation experience, enabling them to focus on visiting the city and making the most of their stay in this exciting coastal location.

ACCOMMODATION OPTIONS

Luxury Hotels

1. The Oysterbox Hotel

Location: 2 Lighthouse Road, Umhlanga Rocks, Durban.

Cost: Starting at $300 per night.

The Oyster Box Hotel, located along the picturesque coastline of Umhlanga Rocks, oozes elegance and refinement at every step. This landmark hotel has stunning views of the Indian Ocean and superb accommodations, featuring spacious rooms and suites decorated with luxurious furniture and modern conveniences. Guests may enjoy world-class cuisine at the hotel's award-winning restaurants, unwind by the infinity pool that overlooks the ocean, or restore their bodies and minds at the luxury spa. The Oyster Box Hotel, with its outstanding service and attention to detail, defines premium hospitality in Durban.

2. The Beverly Hills Hotel.

54 Lighthouse Road in Umhlanga Rocks, Durban.

Cost: Starting at $250 per night

The Beverly Hills Hotel, located in the heart of Umhlanga Rocks, provides discriminating tourists a refuge of sophisticated elegance and incomparable luxury. Each of the hotel's large rooms and suites has modern décor, plush linen, and breathtaking views of the Indian Ocean or beautiful gardens. Guests may dine in elegance in the hotel's famed restaurants, relax with a glass at the rooftop bar, or treat themselves to a variety of decadent spa treatments. With its ideal location and exceptional service, The Beverly Hills Hotel guarantees an enjoyable stay in Durban.

3. The Palace All-Suite

Location: 211 Marine Parade, Durban

Cost: Starting at $200 per night.

Perched on the golden beaches of Durban's famed Golden Mile, The Palace All-Suite provides a magnificent escape in the midst of the city. The hotel's large rooms include modern decor, fully furnished kitchens, and private balconies with panoramic views of the ocean. Guests may relax in luxury at the hotel's outdoor pool and sundeck, eat deliciously at the on-site restaurant, or take advantage of the hotel's handy beachside location to experience Durban's colorful sights and sounds. The Palace All-Suite, with its upmarket facilities and dedicated service, is the ideal choice for a spectacular beach holiday.

4. Royal Palm Hotel

Location: 8 Palm Boulevard, Umhlanga Ridge, Durban.

Cost: Starting at $180 per night.

The Royal Palm Hotel, located in the vibrant Umhlanga Ridge neighborhood, combines contemporary flair with classic charm. The hotel's large suites include sleek modern decor, luxurious beds, and stunning views of the surrounding metropolis. Guests may eat in elegance at the hotel's gourmet restaurant, unwind with a glass at the rooftop bar, or simply relax by the dazzling outdoor pool.

The Royal Palm Hotel, with its central location and upmarket facilities, is an excellent choice for guests looking for elegance and convenience in Durban.

5. The Capitol Pearls

Location: 6 Lagoon Drive, Umhlanga Rocks, Durban.

Cost: Starting at $150 per night

The Capital Pearls, located on the picturesque Umhlanga Promenade, provides tourists with a magnificent beachside getaway with breathtaking views of the Indian Ocean. The hotel's trendy and contemporary apartments provide modern conveniences, fully furnished kitchens, and huge living rooms, giving visitors all the comforts of home. Guests may relax on the hotel's rooftop pool and bar, eat gourmet food at the on-site restaurant, or take a leisurely stroll along the neighboring beach. With its prime location and elegant rooms, The Capital Pearls is an excellent choice for guests looking for a stylish and refined stay in Durban.

Budget Hostels

1. Curiosity Durban

Location: 55 Monty Naicker Road, Durban Central.

Cost: Starting at $15 per night.

Curiocity Durban, located in the heart of Durban's dynamic city center, provides trendy and comfortable accommodations for budget-conscious guests. The hostel offers both dormitory-style and private rooms, each with contemporary conveniences and attractive furniture. Guests may interact and unwind in the hostel's common spaces, which include a rooftop terrace with panoramic views of the downtown skyline. Curiocity Durban's central location and low pricing make it the ideal alternative for budget tourists wishing to enjoy the best of Durban without breaking the bank.

2. Tekweni Backpacker Hostel

Location: 169 Ninth Avenue, Morningside, Durban.

Cost: Starting at $12 per night.

Nestled in the lush neighborhood of Morningside, Tekweni Backpackers Hostel provides budget visitors with a pleasant and inviting environment in which to relax and recharge. The hostel has both dormitory-style and private rooms, both of which have been deliberately constructed to provide visitors with comfort and convenience. Tekweni Backpackers Hostel, with its common kitchen, outdoor swimming pool, and friendly staff, serves as a home away from home for budget-conscious tourists touring Durban.

3. Hippos Hide Backpackers.

Location: 39 Bellevue Road, Kloof, Durban.

Cost: Starting at $10 per night.

Escape the noise and bustle of the city and relax at Hippo Hide Backpackers in Kloof. This low-cost hostel provides dormitory-style accommodation in a tranquil environment surrounded by lush gardens and natural plants. Guests may unwind in the common lounge, prepare meals in the public kitchen, or explore the surrounding nature reserves and hiking paths. Hippo Hide Backpackers, with its inexpensive pricing and calm setting, is the ideal alternative for budget tourists looking for a quiet weekend in Durban.

4. Smith's Cottage

Location: 3-7 8th Avenue, Glenashley, Durban

Cost: Starting at $18 per night.

Smith's Cottage, located in the Glenashley area, provides budget tourists with a nice and comfortable place to stay within a short drive from Durban's city center. The hostel offers both dormitory-style and private rooms, each with basic utilities and comfortable furniture. Guests may unwind in the hostel's community lounge, cook meals in the shared kitchen, or visit surrounding beaches and attractions. Smith's Cottage, with its reasonable pricing and pleasant ambiance, makes an ideal home base for budget-conscious travelers touring Durban.

5. Happy Hippo Accommodation.

Location: 222 Mahatma Gandhi Road, Durban Central.

Cost: Starting at $14 per night.

Happy Hippo Accommodation, located in the heart of Durban's bustling city center, provides budget visitors with a comfortable and cheap location to stay within walking distance of the city's main attractions. The hostel offers both dormitory-style and private rooms, all of which are built for comfort and convenience. Guests may interact with other travelers in the hostel's common spaces, which include a rooftop terrace with views of the metropolitan skyline. Happy Hippo Accommodation, with its central location and affordable pricing, is an excellent alternative for tourists wishing to explore Durban on a shoestring budget.

Bed AND BREAKFASTS

1. The Grange Guest House.

Location: 1 Bute Road, Morningside, Durban.

Cost: Starting at $50 per night

The Grange Guest House, located in the green district of Morningside, provides a delightful bed & breakfast experience in a serene environment. The guest home has nicely designed rooms with modern facilities, including en-suite bathrooms, air conditioning, and flat-screen televisions. Guests may have a great breakfast in the dining room every morning or relax in the lovely garden setting. The Grange Guest House, with its convenient location and customized service, is ideal for guests looking for a calm vacation in Durban.

2. Cowrie Cove Guest House.

Location: 2A Cowrie Road, Umhlanga Rocks, Durban.

Cost: Starting at $60 per night.

Cowrie Cove Guest House, located in the posh enclave of Umhlanga Rocks, provides guests with a magnificent bed & breakfast experience only steps from the beach. The guest house offers tastefully decorated rooms with individual balconies or patios that overlook the ocean, as well as modern facilities like air conditioning, satellite TV, and free Wi-Fi. Guests may begin their day with a tasty breakfast provided on the sunny patio overlooking the pool or unwind in the calm garden setting. Cowrie

Cove Guest House offers a great stay in Durban, thanks to its breathtaking ocean views and excellent service.

3. African Peninsula Guest House.

Location: 54 Marine Drive, Bluff, Durban.

Cost: Starting at $45 per night.

African Peninsula Guest House, perched on a magnificent bluff overlooking the Indian Ocean, provides tourists with a pleasant and inviting bed and breakfast experience in a calm beach location. The guest home has pleasant rooms with contemporary conveniences, including air conditioning, tea/coffee-making facilities, and free Wi-Fi. Every morning, guests may enjoy a full breakfast in the dining room or relax on the patio with breathtaking ocean views. African Peninsula Guest House, with its warm welcome and handy location, is an excellent choice for a quiet break in Durban.

4. Bon Ami Guest House.

Location: 15 Harbor View Avenue, Bluff, Durban.

Cost: Starting at $55 per night.

Bon Ami Guest House, located in the picturesque neighborhood of Bluff, provides tourists with a warm and private bed and breakfast experience while offering breathtaking views of Durban's port and cityscape. The guest home has attractively appointed rooms with contemporary facilities, including en-suite bathrooms, air conditioning, and satellite television. Guests may unwind in the pleasant lounge area or have a great breakfast on the sunny patio overlooking the pool. Bon Ami Guest

House, with its individualized service and gorgeous settings, offers a wonderful stay for visitors to Durban.

5. Emakhosini Boutique Hotel & Conference Center

Location: First Avenue, Morningside, Durban.

Cost: Starting at $70 per night

Emakhosini Boutique Hotel and Conference Centre, conveniently located in the heart of Morningside, provides tourists with a magnificent bed and breakfast experience as well as easy access to Durban's main attractions. The hotel offers attractively designed rooms and suites with modern conveniences such as luxurious bedding, flat-screen TVs, and free Wi-Fi. Guests may have a great breakfast in the dining room every morning or relax in the calm garden setting. Emakhosini Boutique Hotel and Conference Centre offers luxury rooms and excellent service, making it an ideal hideaway for those touring Durban.

TOP ATTRACTIONS IN DURBAN

Beaches And Waterfronts

Durban, located along the scenic Indian Ocean coastline, has a plethora of beautiful beaches and busy waterfront zones that appeal to both inhabitants and tourists. From crowded promenades to quiet stretches of sand, each beach and waterfront region in Durban has its own distinct charm and attractions. Let's get into the specifics of these seaside gems:

1. The Golden Mile, a four-mile stretch of Durban's coastline, is a popular entertainment and leisure hub. The Golden Mile, with its gorgeous beaches, palm-lined promenades, and renowned buildings like the Moses Mabhida Stadium and uShaka Marine World, exemplifies coastal fun and excitement. Visitors may enjoy swimming, surfing, sunbathing, or simply strolling along the waterfront and taking in the bustling scene.

2. uShaka Beach: Located near uShaka Marine World, uShaka Beach offers a peaceful alternative to the busy Golden Mile. This beach's crystal-clear waters and smooth sand make it excellent for swimming, snorkeling, and relaxing with family and friends. Visitors may also visit the adjacent uShaka Marine World, a massive marine theme park including an aquarium, water park, and a variety of entertainment options.

3. South Beach: Located near the southern end of the Golden Mile, South Beach attracts both water sports enthusiasts and sun worshippers. The beach offers

outstanding surfing conditions, with regular waves that draw surfers from all over the world. South Beach also provides a variety of amenities, such as lifeguard stations, beachside eateries, and surfboard and other water sports equipment rentals.

4. North Beach: Located near Suncoast Casino and Entertainment World, North Beach is a popular beach destination in Durban. North Beach's large length of golden sand and calm waves make it ideal for swimming, sunbathing, and beach volleyball. Visitors may also take a stroll down the beachside promenade, which is lined with palm trees and seats affording panoramic views of the ocean.

5. Umhlanga Beach and Pier: Located north of Durban's city center, Umhlanga is an upmarket neighborhood with clean beaches and the historic Umhlanga pier. Umhlanga Beach provides tourists with a peaceful retreat from the city's hustle and bustle, thanks to its quiet seas and breathtaking views of the Indian Ocean. The pier, a prominent landmark, offers a fantastic vantage point for seeing the sunrise or sunset, as well as observing dolphins and whales during the migration season.

Durban's lively waterfront areas complement its gorgeous beaches. The Durban Point Waterfront, for example, is a vibrant collection of restaurants, stores, and entertainment venues set against the background of the harbor. Visitors may enjoy waterfront restaurants, take a gorgeous harbor cruise, or simply relax and admire the city skyline. Durban provides tourists with a variety of coastal experiences, including pristine beaches, bustling promenades, and exciting waterfront zones. Durban's beaches and waterfronts provide something for everyone, whether you want to relax in the sun, participate in exhilarating water sports, or dine on the waterfront. So grab your sunscreen and beach towel and get ready to discover the splendor of Durban's coastal paradise.

Museums And Art Galleries

From immersive historical experiences to modern art exhibitions, Durban has a broad range of cultural institutions waiting to be discovered.

1. Durban Art Gallery: Located in the city center, the Durban Art Gallery showcases South African art from all genres and periods. The gallery houses a large collection of paintings, sculptures, ceramics, and textiles, showcasing the works of both local and foreign artists. Visitors may immerse themselves in the rich tapestry of South African culture and history by viewing the gallery's permanent and changing exhibitions. Admission to the Durban Art Gallery, which is open Tuesday through Sunday from 8:30 AM to 4:00 PM, is free, making it an accessible and engaging cultural experience for everyone.

2. KwaMuhle Museum: Located on Bram Fischer Road in Durban's core business center, the museum explores the city's complicated social and political past. The museum, located in a historic building that originally housed Durban's Native Administration Department, addresses issues of apartheid, urbanization, and resistance via interactive displays, historical documents, and oral histories. The KwaMuhle Museum is open Monday through Saturday from 8:30 a.m. to 4:00 p.m. Admission is reasonable, with discounts available for students and seniors. Visitors may obtain a better knowledge of Durban's past and present by engaging in thought-provoking exhibitions and multimedia presentations.

3. Phansi Museum: Located in Glenwood, the Phansi Museum showcases South Africa's diverse cultural traditions. The museum, housed in a renovated Victorian

home, displays a large collection of African art, crafts, and antiques, such as traditional Zulu beading, carved wooden masks, and ceremonial items. The Phansi Museum is open by appointment only and offers guided tours conducted by qualified docents who explain the cultural importance and workmanship of each exhibit. Visitors may also stroll around the museum's serene grounds and watch traditional music and dance performances during special occasions.

4. The BAT Centre: Located on Durban's Victoria Embankment, this cultural hub promotes local artists and entrepreneurs. The center includes galleries, studios, and performance spaces that showcase the work of KwaZulu-Natal's emerging and renowned artists. Visitors may peruse a wide range of modern artworks, see live music and dance performances, or take part in workshops and artisan fairs. With its gorgeous waterfront setting and vibrant programming, The BAT Centre provides a one-of-a-kind and immersive cultural experience for guests of all ages.

5. The Old House Museum: Located in Berea, this museum preserves the interiors of a magnificent Victorian home, providing a look into Durban's colonial history. Built-in the late nineteenth century, the museum transports visitors back in time with period furnishings, antique décor, and Victorian-era items. Guided tours of the museum give intriguing insights into the life of Durban's early inhabitants, while the adjacent gardens provide a peaceful respite from the city's hustle and bustle. The Old House Museum is open Tuesday through Sunday from 10:00 a.m. to 4:00 p.m., and entry is reasonably priced, making it a must-see site for both history buffs and cultural adventurers.

Explore Durban's intriguing museums and art galleries, each giving a distinct perspective on the city's tradition and creativity. Whether you're a history buff, an art lover, or just a curious visitor, Durban's cultural institutions offer a satisfying and instructive experience for everyone who visits.

Wildlife Parks And Reserves

Durban, located in the heart of KwaZulu-Natal province, serves as a gateway to a world rich in natural beauty and wildlife. Explore the region's wildlife parks and reserves, where you may see a wide variety of flora and fauna in their natural environments. From famous safari experiences to fascinating conservation initiatives, here's a detailed guide to Durban's wildlife parks and reserves.

1. Hluhluwe-iMfolozi Park is located at 236 Main Road in Hluhluwe, KwaZulu-Natal.

Daily, 6:00 AM - 6:00 PM.

Cost: Entrance fees vary according to age and nationality

Hluhluwe-iMfolozi Park, one of Africa's oldest designated game reserves, is a wildlife enthusiast's heaven. This park, which covers over 96,000 hectares, is well-known for its conservation efforts, notably those aimed at saving the endangered white rhinoceros. Visitors may go on self-drive safaris or guided game drives to see the Big Five (lion, elephant, buffalo, rhinoceros, and leopard), as well as a variety of other animal species, including giraffes, zebras, and cheetahs. For individuals who want to immerse themselves in nature, the park has walking routes, picnic areas, and lodging alternatives.

2. Tala Private Game Reserve is located at R603, Tala Valley, in Camperdown, KwaZulu-Natal.

Daily, 7:30 AM - 5:00 PM.

Cost: Entrance costs vary according to age and activity.

Tala Private Game Reserve, located an hour's drive from Durban, provides an accessible getaway into the heart of nature. This 3,000-hectare reserve is home to a wide variety of animals, including rhinos, hippos, giraffes, and more than 380 bird species. Visitors may participate in guided game drives, bush walks, and birding expeditions supervised by trained rangers. Tala also has exquisite lodging alternatives, such as safari lodges and tented camps, where tourists may rest and unwind amidst the splendor of the African bush.

3. Umgeni River Bird Park is located at 490 Riverside Road in Durban North, KwaZulu-Natal.

Daily, 9:00 AM - 5:00 PM.

Cost: Entrance costs vary according to age.

The Umgeni River Bird Park in Durban is a must-see site for both bird aficionados and wildlife lovers. This park, located along the banks of the Umgeni River, is home to more than 800 bird species from across the world, including parrots, hornbills, and flamingos. Visitors may explore the lush aviaries and groomed gardens, getting up close and personal with these wonderful feathery animals. Daily bird demonstrations and feeding sessions educate and amuse guests of all ages.

4. Crocworld Conservation Centre: Located at 2 Crocworld Conservation Centre in Scottburgh, KwaZulu-Natal.

Daily, 8:00 AM - 4:30 PM.

Cost: Entrance fees vary by age.

Crocworld Conservation Centre, located south of Durban on the gorgeous South Coast, provides a unique chance to learn about South Africa's crocodile population and other reptile species. The facility has educational displays, guided tours, and regular crocodile feedings, allowing visitors to see these prehistoric beasts up close. In addition to crocodiles, Crocworld is home to a variety of indigenous and exotic animals, such as snakes, tortoises, and birds of prey. The complex also has a lovely walking track, picnic spots, and a restaurant that serves wonderful meals with a view.

5. PheZulu Safari Park is located on Old Main Road in Botha's Hill, KwaZulu-Natal.

Open daily from 9:00 AM until 4:30 PM.

Cost: Entrance costs vary according to age and activity.

PheZulu Safari Park, perched above the Valley of a Thousand Hills, provides tourists with a view of KwaZulu-Natal's rich cultural legacy and natural splendor. The park provides guided tours of traditional Zulu homesteads, where visitors may learn about Zulu customs, rituals, and crafts. The park's main attraction is the thrilling crocodile and snake exhibitions, in which skilled handlers demonstrate these intriguing reptiles in action. PheZulu also provides game drives into surrounding game reserves, where visitors may see local species like zebras, wildebeests, and antelope.

OUTDOOR ADVENTURES

Surfing And Watersports

Durban, surrounded by the warm waters of the Indian Ocean, is a watersports enthusiast's dream, with a wealth of exciting activities for people of all ages and ability levels. Everyone may enjoy surfing the legendary Durban waves or discovering the underwater world through snorkeling and diving. Let's get into the specifics of these exciting watersports excursions.

1. Surfing: Durban's beaches provide world-class waves, attracting surfers from all over the world. Whether you're a seasoned veteran or a newbie trying to catch your first wave, there are several surf places to pick from. The beaches of the Golden Mile, including North and South Beach, have steady surfable waves. Surfboard rentals are offered at many surf shops around the shore, with rates ranging from $10 to $20 per hour. For those new to the sport, expert teachers provide individualized coaching and tuition to help you learn the art of surfing.

2. Kiteboarding: Kiteboarding is ideal for adrenaline-fueled watersports enthusiasts. Durban's regular winds and wide-open beaches make for perfect kiteboarding conditions. Several kiteboarding schools and rental businesses along the shore provide equipment rentals, instruction, and guided tours. Kiteboarding courses normally cost $50 to $100 per hour, depending on the duration and degree of training. Experienced instructors give customized coaching, teaching participants the fundamentals of kite control, board handling, and safety regulations to ensure a safe and pleasurable time on the water.

3. Stand-Up Paddleboarding (SUP): SUP is a unique way to explore Durban's coastline while getting full-body exercise. SUP rentals are offered at a variety of seaside locales, with rates generally ranging from $15 to $30 per hour. Beginners may take beginning classes to master the fundamentals of paddling technique and balance, while expert paddlers can join guided SUP trips around the gorgeous coastline. Whether you're floating across calm seas or surfing modest waves, stand-up paddleboarding is a fun and absorbing way to connect with nature while being active on the water.

4. Snorkeling and Scuba Diving: Discover the vivid underwater world of Durban's marine reserves with snorkeling and scuba diving excursions. The warm waters of the Indian Ocean are filled with vibrant coral reefs, tropical fish, and other marine life waiting to be explored. Several dive firms provide guided snorkeling and scuba diving tours to prominent dive destinations, including Aliwal Shoal and Sodwana Bay. Prices for guided diving tours vary based on location, duration, and equipment rental fees, with full-day excursions often costing between $50 and $150 per person. Experienced dive instructors give detailed briefings and safety instructions, providing a memorable and safe underwater experience for divers of all ability levels.

5. Durban offers thrilling water sports such as jet skiing and parasailing. Jet ski rentals are provided at many beachside spots, allowing riders to jet across the waves and explore the shore at their leisure. Jet ski rentals normally cost $50 to $100 per half-hour, with reductions available for longer rentals. Parasailing excursions provide a bird's-eye perspective of Durban's gorgeous coastline as participants soar far above the water while

connected to a parachute carried by a speedboat. Prices for parasailing adventures vary based on the time and height of the trip, with possibilities for both solo and tandem flights. Experienced instructors and operators offer a safe and exhilarating experience for participants, making jet skiing and parasailing popular among Durban watersports fans.

Hiking Trails

Whether you choose to take a leisurely stroll or a strenuous hike, Durban's hiking trails provide breathtaking landscapes, diverse animals, and an opportunity to reconnect with nature. Let's look at some of the most intriguing hiking routes in Durban:

1. Krantzkloof Nature Reserve: Located in the Valley of a Thousand Hills, Krantzkloof Nature Reserve offers a vast network of hiking paths through lush indigenous woods, tumbling waterfalls, and stunning gorges. The paths are suitable for all fitness levels, ranging from short walks to more demanding climbs, such as the Valley Trail, which provides stunning views from the edge of the valley. The reserve's day visiting costs range from $2 to $4 per person, making it an economical alternative for wildlife enthusiasts of all ages.

2. Kloof Gorge Trail: Located in Kloof, hikers may enjoy panoramic views of the Umgeni River and surrounding scenery throughout the trail. This fairly tough walk winds through lush forests, rocky outcrops, and peaceful streams, providing possibilities for birding and animal observation along the way. The route is free to use and ideal for intermediate hikers seeking a pleasurable outdoor experience.

3. Umhlanga Lagoon Nature Reserve offers coastal hiking routes through dune woods, marshes, and scenic beaches. The Beachwood Mangrove Trail is a popular alternative for a leisurely stroll through a protected mangrove forest, complete with informational signs emphasizing the value of this unique environment. The reserve's entrance is free,

making it an excellent choice for a low-cost outdoor excursion.

4. Inanda Dam and Resort: Located near Durban, hikers may enjoy magnificent routes with panoramic views of the dam and adjacent slopes. The Inanda Mountain Trail is a strenuous climb that takes around 3-4 hours to complete, taking hikers through steep terrain and unique bushveld. Hikers will see a variety of bird species along the path, as well as small animals like duikers and vervet monkeys. The resort is reasonably priced, with day visitors paying between $2 and $4 per person.

5. Giba Gorge Mountain Bike Park: In addition to mountain biking, the park has picturesque hiking paths for outdoor enthusiasts. The routes run through gorgeous settings, including indigenous woods, grassy slopes, and rocky outcrops, giving hikers a variety of hard terrain to explore. Hikers may enjoy breathtaking views of the gorge and surrounding farmland, with chances to see animals along the route. Admission to the park is reasonable, with day passes available for $2 per person.

Conclusion: Durban's hiking routes provide different outdoor experiences for nature enthusiasts and adventure seekers, from rocky mountain trails to beach walks. With low admission fees and breathtaking scenery, these trails offer the ideal chance to escape the hustle and bustle of the city and immerse yourself in the grandeur of South Africa's natural surroundings. So strap up your hiking boots, grab your water bottle, and prepare for an incredible trekking excursion in Durban.

Safari Tours

From the magnificent Big Five to the rich birds and beautiful scenery, Durban has safari alternatives to suit any traveler's interests. Let's go into the details of some interesting safari trips in Durban.

1. Safari in Hluhluwe-iMfolozi Park: Led by skilled guides, explore Africa's oldest wildlife reserve. This park is home to a rich assortment of animals, including the Big Five, cheetahs, and wild dogs, and it provides exhilarating game drives through its unspoiled wilderness. Tours normally run for 3-4 hours, giving plenty of time for animal encounters and photo opportunities. Safari tour prices vary according to time and number of participants, with possibilities for both group and private tours.

2. Phinda Private Game Reserve Safari: For a unique safari experience, explore Phinda Private Game Reserve, located just a few hours' drive from Durban. This magnificent reserve provides guided game drives in open-air safari vehicles, giving visitors unmatched opportunities to see rare and endangered animals, including black rhinos and African wild dogs. Safari tours in Phinda normally last from half to full days, with fees starting at about $200 per person. Guests may also choose from immersive walking safaris or boat excursions around the reserve's canals for an amazing wildlife experience.

3. Tala Private Game Reserve Safari: Located near Durban, Tala Private Game Reserve provides a convenient way to see the African wild without leaving the city. Guided game drives across the reserve's different ecosystems offer the opportunity to see giraffes, zebras,

and a variety of antelope. Safari trips at Tala run around 2-3 hours and are led by skilled rangers who give information about the reserve's animals and conservation activities. Tala's safari experiences start at around $50 per person, with discounts available for children and parties.

4. Explore KwaZulu-Natal's cultural legacy and natural beauty with a safari excursion at PheZulu Safari Park. Located in the Valley of a Thousand Hills, this park provides guided game drives through picturesque landscapes rich with species such as zebras, wildebeests, and giraffes. Visitors may also participate in cultural events such as traditional Zulu dances and village visits, which offer a unique glimpse into the native way of life. Safari trips at PheZulu Safari Park run around 2 hours and are reasonably priced, making them accessible to guests of all budgets.

5. Safari Tour in Oribi Gorge Nature Reserve: Explore the reserve's magnificent scenery and diverse wildlife. Guided game drives across the reserve provide possibilities to see elusive animals like leopards, as well as a variety of birds and smaller mammals. Tours often include pauses at panoramic vistas overlooking the gorge, where guests may see the breathtaking natural surroundings. Safari trips in Oribi Gorge Nature Reserve vary in length and cost, with options for both half-day and full-day excursions.

CULINARY DELIGHTS

Traditional South African Cuisine

Enjoy the rich and tasty world of traditional South African food during your vacation to Durban. From substantial stews to savory meats and sweet desserts, Durban has a wide range of culinary pleasures that represent the country's rich cultural past. Let's have a look at some of the must-try classic South African meals in Durban:

1. Bunny Chow at Jeera Restaurant (Suncoast Boulevard, Durban)

Cost: $8 to $12 per serving.

At Jeera Restaurant, indulge in a famous Durban delicacy, Bunny Chow. This renowned meal, which originated in the Indian population of Durban, is made out of a hollowed-out loaf of bread filled with savory curry. Choose from a range of fillings, such as chicken, lamb, or vegetarian, and enjoy the aromatic spices and delicate meat or veggies. Jeera Restaurant takes a new approach to this classic dish, offering it with a side of sambals and pickles for a blast of flavor in every bite.

2. Bobotie at The Africa Café (234 Anton Lembede Street, Durban)

Cost: $10 to $15 for each serving.

Bobotie, a South African comfort meal, may be enjoyed at The Africa Café. This traditional meal comprises spicy minced meat, usually beef or lamb, combined with dried fruit, nuts, and a creamy egg custard topping. The Africa Café updates this classic recipe with robust flavors and locally sourced ingredients. Bobotie served with aromatic yellow rice and chutney, is a must-try meal for anybody looking to experience real South African cuisine in Durban.

3. Barbeque (Braai) at Moyo Ushaka Pier:

Location: Moyo Ushaka Pier, 1 Bell Street, Durban.

Cost: $20 to $30 per person.

Experience the South African custom of braai, or BBQ, at Moyo Ushaka Pier. Nestled along Durban's beachfront, this bustling restaurant provides a one-of-a-kind dining experience with breathtaking views of the Indian Ocean. Enjoy a variety of grilled meats, including juicy steaks, boerewors sausages, and peri-peri chicken, all cooked to perfection over an open flame. A braai at Moyo Ushaka Pier is a savory celebration of South African culinary history, served with traditional side dishes such as pap (maize porridge) and chakalaka (spicy relish).

4. Malva Pudding in The Oyster Box Hotel:

Location: The Oyster Box Hotel, 2 Lighthouse Road, Umhlanga, Durban.

Cost: $8 to $12 per serving.

The Oyster Box Hotel serves Malva Pudding, a delicious dessert. This popular South African delicacy is a rich and spongy sponge cake flavored with apricot jam and covered with a sweet and sticky caramel sauce. Malva Pudding served warm with a dab of vanilla ice cream or custard, is the ideal way to finish a fantastic dinner. Indulge in this classic pleasure while admiring the magnificent ambiance and seaside views at The Oyster Box Hotel.

5. Durban Curry, Capsicum Restaurant:

Capsicum Restaurant is located at 90 Fairway Drive, Durban North.

Cost: $15 to $20 for each dish.

Capsicum Restaurant serves Durban Curry, which captures the tastes of Durban's lively Indian community. Durban Curry, known for its robust spices and spicy heat, is a gastronomic treat that has come to represent the city's eclectic cuisine culture. Capsicum Restaurant serves a variety of curry dishes, from conventional chicken or lamb curry to vegetarian choices, all bursting with aromatic aromas and served with fluffy rice or buttery naan bread. Capsicum Restaurant serves real Durban curry and takes you on a gastronomic trip through the city's rich traditions.

Fusion Restaurants

At these one-of-a-kind Durban eateries, traditional South African foods meet global influences to create a gourmet blend of tastes and cultures. These fusion restaurants provide a unique eating experience, with Asian-inspired meals and European twists on local favorites. Let's consider each option:

1. Mali Fusion Restaurant is located at 23 Mackeurtan Avenue, Durban North.

Opening hours: Tuesday through Sunday, 12:00 PM to 10:00 PM.

Mali Fusion Restaurant, located in the heart of Durban North, fuses Africa's rich tastes with Asian and European culinary traditions. Mali's cuisine, created by award-winning chefs, features a broad choice of fusion meals, including seafood sushi rolls with a South African twist and delectable curries flavored with unique spices. The restaurant's elegant and modern environment creates the ideal atmosphere for a wonderful dining experience, whether you're having a leisurely brunch or a romantic supper.

2. The Chef's Table location: 54 Lighthouse Road, Umhlanga Rocks, Durban.

Opening hours: Monday through Sunday, 12:00 PM to 10:00 PM.

The Chef's Table, located in the upmarket neighborhood of Umhlanga Rocks, provides a unique fusion dining experience that highlights the diversity of South African cuisine. Chef Kayla-Ann Osborn leads the restaurant, which serves a cuisine inspired by African, Asian, and

European flavors, including ostrich carpaccio with truffle aioli and coconut-infused crab curry. The Chef's Table also has a well-chosen wine selection spanning local and international vintages, allowing customers to enjoy the ideal combination with their meal.

3. Unity Brasserie & Bar is located at 35 Montgomery Drive in Athlone, Durban.

Opening Hours: Monday-Saturday, 11:30 AM - 11:00 PM

Unity Brasserie & Bar, in the lovely neighborhood of Athlone, offers a gourmet tour throughout the world. Unity's menu combines aspects of French, Italian, and South African cuisine, delighting the senses with powerful tastes and imaginative presentations. From gourmet pizzas topped with local biltong to fusion tapas plates featuring the finest of global ingredients, Unity Brasserie & Bar is the ideal place for foodies looking for an exceptional dining experience in Durban.

4. The Chairman's address: 146 Mahatma Gandhi Road, Point, Durban.

Opening hours: Thursday-Saturday, 6:00 PM - 12:00 AM

The Chairman, located in Durban's lively Point district, offers a one-of-a-kind dining experience that combines music, art, and gastronomy. This unusual restaurant and jazz bar has a fusion menu that combines African, Asian, and Middle Eastern tastes, including Moroccan-spiced lamb sliders and Cape Malay chicken curry. The Chairman's sophisticated and intimate environment sets the stage for an evening of gastronomic discovery and live entertainment.

5. Oki's Daruma, located at 170 Florida Road in Morningside, Durban

Opening hours: Monday through Sunday, 12:00 PM to 9:00 PM.

Daruma by Oki, located on popular Florida Road in Morningside, serves Japanese cuisine with a South African twist. This fusion restaurant mixes traditional Japanese cooking techniques with locally obtained ingredients to produce unique meals that entice the palate. Daruma by Oki provides a gastronomic journey that embraces the best of both worlds, with sushi rolls infused with Durban's famous peri-peri sauce and ramen bowls with locally caught fish.

Street Food Hotspots

Durban's street food culture is a taste melting pot, combining local favorites with foreign influences to create an unforgettable gastronomic trip. From fragrant curries to delectable seafood meals, the city's street food hotspots provide a delicious variety of alternatives for foodies to discover. Let's explore the colorful world of street food in Durban.

1. Victoria Street Market: Located at 151 Victoria Street, Durban Central

Monday-Saturday, 8:00 AM to 5:00 PM.

Victoria Street Market is a lively center of activity that must be seen by anybody looking for true Durban street cuisine. Visitors may enjoy a sensory feast at the market, which includes aromatic spices and freshly cooked delicacies. Samoosas, bunny chows, and rotis are typical Indian treats, but you can also have local favorites like boerewors rolls and bunny burgers. Victoria Street Market is a foodie's dream, thanks to its bustling atmosphere and numerous gastronomic offers.

2. The Workshop Shopping Centre Food Market is located at 99 Samora Machel Street, Durban Central.

Opening Hours: Friday-Sunday, 10:00 AM - 10:00 PM

The Workshop Shopping Centre Food Market offers a dynamic venue in which to sample Durban's international cuisine. This colorful outdoor market has a wide variety of food vendors providing everything from traditional South African delicacies to worldwide favorites. Indulge in delicious burgers, handcrafted pizzas, and delectable street cuisine snacks while taking in the lively atmosphere. The Workshop Food Market, which features live music and entertainment, is ideal for a casual eating experience with friends and family.

3. Durban Beachfront Promenade - Marine Parade, Durban Beachfront.

Opening Hours: 24/7

Take a leisurely stroll down Durban's famed beachfront promenade to enjoy a plethora of street cuisine delicacies. From vendors selling freshly grilled seafood to mobile carts serving traditional South African foods, the promenade is a foodie's dream. Enjoy freshly shucked oysters, spicy grilled prawns, and savory fish and chips while admiring panoramic views of the ocean. The Durban Beachfront Promenade, with its calm attitude and gorgeous beachfront background, is ideal for savoring the city's tastes.

4. Florida Road Food Market: Located at 267 Florida Road, Morningside, Durban.

Wednesday through Sunday, 5:00 PM to 10:00 PM.

The Florida Road Food Market captures the bright spirit of Durban's famous Florida Road. This lively night market has a vast array of food vendors serving a variety of gastronomic pleasures. From gourmet burgers and wood-fired pizzas to genuine Durban curries and delectable desserts, there's something to satisfy every appetite. Take a seat at one of the communal tables, sip artisan beers or cocktails, and soak up the bustling ambiance of this famous street food spot.

5. Warwick Junction Market: Located at 170 Queen Street, Durban Central.

Opening hours: Monday-Saturday, 6:00 AM - 6:00 PM

Visit Warwick Junction Market, one of Durban's oldest and largest informal markets, to immerse yourself in the city's bustling street food culture. There's a bewildering selection of food stalls and sellers selling anything from traditional Zulu cuisine to spicy Indian street food. Biltong, samoosas, and rabbit chows are popular meals, but you may also enjoy strange treats like fried insects and offal. Warwick Junction Market's lively atmosphere and unique tastes provide a true experience of Durban's rich culinary history.

NIGHTLIFE AND ENTERTAINMENT

Bars And Clubs

Durban pulsates with vitality when the sun goes down, with a broad selection of bars and clubs where residents and visitors can relax, dance, and interact. From stylish cocktail bars to throbbing nightclubs, these are some of the most popular places to experience Durban's nightlife:

1. The Chairman's location is 146 Mahatma Gandhi Road, Point, Durban.

Opening hours: Thursday-Saturday, 6:00 PM - 12:00 AM

Tucked away in Durban's busy Point district, The Chairman stands out as a dynamic hotspot for live music and inventive drinks. With its small location and creative design, this jazz bar radiates refinement while retaining a relaxed environment. Patrons may sip carefully made beverages while listening to local jazz bands and international musicians. Whether you're a music fan or simply looking for a fashionable place to chill, The Chairman guarantees an amazing night out.

2. Tiger's Milk location: 15 Browns Road, Point Waterfront, Durban.

Monday through Sunday, 11:00 AM to 2:00 AM.

Tiger's Milk, located in the heart of Durban's Point Waterfront neighborhood, serves a dynamic combination of outstanding cuisine, artisan beer, and live sports screens. This stylish bar and café has a large outdoor terrace with panoramic views of the port, making it perfect for sundowners and informal parties. Guests may enjoy scrumptious burgers, pizzas, and bar snacks while experiencing a wide range of local and foreign beers on tap. Tiger's Milk, with its vibrant environment and polite service, is a popular choice for both residents and visitors.

3. Beach Bums Restaurant & Bar: Located at 65 Casuarina Beach Road, Westbrook, Durban.

Monday through Sunday, 9:00 AM to 10:00 PM.

Beach Bums Restaurant & Bar, located in the seaside hamlet of Westbrook, offers a relaxed beachside atmosphere. This dynamic location provides a relaxing ambiance in which guests may relax with a chilled drink in hand while enjoying the sun and sea wind. Beach Bums serves a wide range of beverages, from pleasant drinks to ice-cold beers. The pub usually organizes live music concerts and beach parties, which contribute to the celebratory atmosphere. Whether you're looking for a relaxing lunch or a lively night out by the sea, Beach Bums guarantees an unforgettable experience.

4. Views From Twenty5:

Location: 25 Silver Avenue, Stamford Hill, Durban.

Opening hours: Wednesday-Sunday, 4:00 PM - 12:00 AM

Views At Twenty5, located atop the historic Moses Mabhida Stadium, provide unsurpassed panoramic views of Durban's skyline and beaches. This rooftop bar and lounge offers a refined environment for drinks, with beautiful design and ambient lighting providing an appealing atmosphere. Guests may enjoy handmade beverages created by experienced mixologists, as well as a carefully chosen assortment of tapas and light nibbles. Whether you're celebrating a special event or simply relaxing after a long day, Views At Twenty5 provides a sumptuous respite from the rush and bustle of the city below.

5. Absolute Bar: Located at 130 Florida Road, Morningside, Durban

Opening Hours: Monday-Sunday, 5:00 PM-2:00 AM

Absolute Bar, located in the busy Florida Road strip in Morningside, is a popular spot for cocktails, music, and dancing. This sleek and modern venue has a trendy interior with plush seats and cutting-edge sound and lighting equipment, offering the ideal setting for a night out on the town. The bar offers a diverse assortment of specialty cocktails, premium spirits, and wines, so there's something for everyone. Absolute Bar's vibrant atmosphere and enthusiastic audience provide an amazing evening experience in Durban.

Live Music Venues

From quiet jazz clubs to vibrant concert venues, Durban has a wide range of alternatives for music lovers to enjoy. Here are some of the city's must-see live music venues.

1. The Jazzy Rainbow is located at 93 Smiso Nkwanyana Road in Morningside, Durban.

Opening Hours: Tuesday through Saturday, 5:00 PM to 12:00 AM.

The Jazzy Rainbow, located in the heart of Morningside, is a charming jazz club that embraces South Africa's rich musical legacy. This compact venue features frequent live concerts by excellent local jazz artists, offering an immersive experience for both jazz fans and casual listeners. The Jazzy Rainbow, with its warm environment and outstanding acoustics, is the ideal location for enjoying soulful songs and smooth rhythms while sipping handmade drinks or eating a light lunch.

2. The Winston Pub is located at 9 Clark Road in Glenwood, Durban.

Opening hours: Monday-Sunday, 6:00 PM - 2:00 AM

The Winston Pub in Durban's bustling Glenwood district is a must-see for fans of the city's alternative music scene. For decades, this historic venue has hosted live performances by new artists and established bands from a variety of genres, including punk, rock, indie, and electronic. The Winston Pub's laid-back ambiance and reasonable beverages make it a popular gathering area for music fans wanting to discover new talent and enjoy live music in an intimate environment.

3. Zack's Wilson's Wharf location: Shop 1, 14 Boatmans Road, Durban.

Monday through Sunday, 11:00 AM to 10:00 PM.

Zack's Wilson's Wharf, located on Durban's scenic waterfront, provides a one-of-a-kind live music experience while also providing spectacular harbor views. This lively facility has live bands and solo performers that play a wide range of musical genres, including jazz, blues, and reggae. Guests may unwind on the outside deck or enjoy the lively ambiance inside while sampling fresh seafood and creative beverages. Zack's Wilson's Wharf is the ideal spot for a fantastic night out with friends or family, thanks to its energetic entertainment and picturesque setting.

4. The Barnyard Theatre is located at Suncoast Boulevard, Suncoast Casino, Durban.

Opening hours vary depending on the performance schedule.

Experience the excitement of live entertainment at The Barnyard Theatre, which is part of the Suncoast Casino complex in Durban. This top entertainment facility presents a diverse selection of live music acts, including tribute shows, comedy evenings, and musical revues, with brilliant artists from all across South Africa. The Barnyard Theatre, with its cutting-edge sound and lighting equipment, comfortable seating, and expansive stage, provides an outstanding experience for audiences of all ages. Whether you prefer rock, pop, or country music, The Barnyard Theatre has something for everyone.

5. The Plant:

Location: 5 Station Drive in Durban.

Thursday-Saturday, 4:00 PM to 12:00 AM.

The Plant, located on Station Drive in Durban, is a hip and diverse venue that presents frequent live music events, including both local and touring musicians. This stylish establishment, housed in a converted warehouse, exudes industrial chic with exposed brick walls, comfy lounging spaces, and a laid-back attitude. Guests may enjoy performances by performers from a variety of genres, including acoustic folk, indie rock, electronic, and experimental music. The Plant, with its inventive drinks, artisan brews, and varied music roster, is a must-see location for music fans looking for a one-of-a-kind and unforgettable experience in Durban's live music scene.

Theatres And Cinemas

Discover the colorful world of stage performances and blockbuster movies at Durban's leading theaters and cinemas. Whether you enjoy theater or movies, these locations provide something for everyone. Let's look into each option:

1. Elizabeth Sneddon Theatre is located on Mazisi Kunene Road at the University of KwaZulu-Natal in Durban.

Opening hours vary depending on the performance schedule.

The Elizabeth Sneddon Theatre, located on the University of KwaZulu-Natal campus, is a major location for live events and theatrical plays in Durban. The theatre, named after the great South African writer Elizabeth Sneddon, features a variety of entertainment, such as plays, musicals, dance performances, and comedy acts. The Elizabeth Sneddon Theatre, with its cutting-edge technology and comfortable seating, offers an immersive experience for spectators of all ages. Whether you're watching a thought-provoking drama or a family-friendly musical, this renowned theater in Durban provides world-class entertainment.

2. The Playhouse Theatre is located at 29 Anton Lembede Street, Durban.

Opening hours vary depending on the performance schedule.

The Playhouse Theatre, located in the heart of Durban's central business area, is a cultural monument that hosts a wide variety of performing arts shows. The Playhouse

Theatre hosts a diverse range of events throughout the year, including grand opera performances, contemporary dance acts, and theatrical plays. The main theater, with its sumptuous design and vast seating, provides an exquisite environment for live performances, while the smaller theaters are intimate locations for experimental theater and developing performers. The Playhouse Theatre, with its rich history and dedication to creative excellence, is a must-see site for theater aficionados in Durban.

3. Suncoast CineCentre: Located at Suncoast Boulevard, Suncoast Casino, Durban.

Monday through Sunday, 10:00 AM to 11:00 PM.

Experience the enchantment of the silver screen at Suncoast CineCentre, which is part of the Suncoast Casino complex in Durban. Suncoast CineCentre provides moviegoers with an exceptional cinematic experience, with cutting-edge projection and sound systems, comfortable seats, and a broad selection of films. From Hollywood blockbusters to independent films and foreign releases, the theater offers a diverse selection of films across many genres. Guests may also get food and refreshments from the concession stand, making it an ideal spot for a movie night with friends or family.

4. Nu Metro Cornubia Mall is located on Flanders Drive in Mount Edgecombe, Durban.

Opening Hours: Monday-Sunday, 10:00 AM - 10:00 PM

Nu Metro Cinemas, located inside the popular Cornubia Mall in Mount Edgecombe, provides a modern and pleasant movie-going experience for people of all ages. The theater has cutting-edge displays and sound equipment, as well as a varied collection of films ranging from action blockbusters to family favorites. With its accessible location and enough seating, Nu Metro Cornubia Mall offers a peaceful setting for moviegoers to experience the newest blockbusters on the big screen. Whether you attend a matinee or an evening movie, Nu Metro Cinemas guarantees an amazing cinematic experience in Durban.

5. Ster-Kinekor Gateway Theatre of Shopping: Located at 1 Palm Boulevard, Umhlanga Ridge, Durban.

Monday through Sunday, 9:00 AM to 10:00 PM.

Ster-Kinekor Cinema, located within the renowned Gateway Theatre of Shopping in Umhlanga Ridge, provides a superior movie-watching experience for cinephiles. Ster-Kinekor Cinema, with its state-of-the-art screens, sumptuous seats, and cutting-edge technology, offers an immersive cinematic experience that takes spectators into action. The theater shows a broad range of films, including 3D and IMAX movies, so there's something for everyone. Guests may also enjoy delicious food and drinks from the concession stand, making it an ideal location for a night at the movies.

SHOPPING IN DURBAN

Markets And Bazaars

Durban's colorful marketplaces and bazaars provide a unique opportunity to experience the city's rich culture, cuisine, and crafts. From lively street markets to artisanal bazaars, each site offers a diverse range of colors, flavors, and customs. Here's a complete reference to some of the best marketplaces and bazaars in Durban:

1. Victoria Street Market: Located at 151/155 Victoria Street, Durban.

Monday through Saturday, 8:00 AM to 5:00 PM; Sunday, 9:00 AM to 4:00 PM.

At the historic Victoria Street Market, you'll find exotic spices, vibrant textiles, and handcrafted goods. This old market, located in Durban's Indian Quarter, is a veritable treasure trove of South African and Indian pleasures. Wander through the labyrinthine lanes filled with vendors offering everything from fresh vegetables and seafood to traditional attire, jewelry, and gifts. The market's food court offers typical Durban cuisine, including aromatic curries, samoosas, and bunny chows. Victoria Street Market, with its colorful ambiance and numerous offers, is a must-see destination for both shoppers and foodies.

2. Morning Trade Market: Location: 15 Station Drive, Durban.

Opening hours: Sunday, 8:00 AM - 1:00 PM.

Experience the finest of Durban's artisanal food and craft culture at The Morning Trade Market, which takes place every Sunday in the stylish Station Drive neighborhood. This colorful market features a carefully chosen collection of local producers, farmers, and craftsmen, selling a variety of fresh vegetables, gourmet delicacies, artisanal items, and handcrafted crafts. Browse around stalls selling organic fruits and veggies, artisanal bread, cheeses, and pastries, as well as one-of-a-kind handcrafted jewelry, clothes, and home décor. Grab a coffee or freshly squeezed juice from one of the market's sellers, then explore this vibrant community hub while listening to live music and entertainment.

3. The Stables Lifestyle Market is located at 9 Jaco Jackson Drive, Durban North.

Wednesday through Friday, 5:00 PM to 9:00 PM; Saturday and Sunday, 9:00 AM to 5:00 PM.

The Stables Lifestyle Market, located in the green neighborhood of Durban North, provides a delightful combination of handcrafted items, gourmet dining, and family-friendly entertainment. This lively market, housed in a converted stableyard, offers a wide variety of booths selling homemade jewelry, apparel, art, and decor, as well as fresh vegetables, baked products, and specialized cuisines. Take a leisurely stroll around the market's lovely settings, peruse the unique items, and savor tasty delicacies from the food sellers. The Stables Lifestyle Market is ideal for a weekend getaway with family and friends, thanks to its relaxing atmosphere and diverse range of activities for all ages.

4. Essenwood Craft Market: Located in Berea Park, Essenwood Road, Durban.

Opening hours: Saturday, 9:00 AM - 2:00 PM

Essenwood Craft Market, located in picturesque Berea Park, is a favorite weekend attraction for both locals and tourists. This colorful market features a wide variety of handcrafted crafts, artworks, and artisanal items manufactured by local craftsmen and crafters. Browse around stalls selling one-of-a-kind jewelry, ceramics, woodwork, textiles, and other items while listening to live music and entertainment in the park. As you tour the Essenwood Craft Market, you may sample excellent street cuisine from the sellers, enjoy freshly made coffee, and take up the bustling ambiance.

5. Durban Botanic Gardens Market is located at 9A John Zikhali Road in Berea, Durban.

Opening hours: Sunday, 9:00 AM - 2:00 PM.

The Durban Botanic Gardens Market, which takes place on the last Sunday of each month, combines the beauty of nature with the excitement of shopping. Set against the background of the city's oldest botanical gardens, this lovely market provides a delectable mix of handmade goods, organic vegetables, and garden-related items. Stroll around the beautiful foliage, shop kiosks selling homemade crafts, jewelry, plants, and flowers, and watch live music and entertainment. The Durban Botanic Gardens Market, with its scenic location and numerous wares, offers visitors of all ages a calm respite as well as a one-of-a-kind shopping experience.

Shopping Malls

Discover a world of retail therapy and entertainment at Durban's best shopping malls, where you can shop, dine, and relax all in one location. From premium shops to big retail brands, each mall provides a one-of-a-kind shopping experience based on your interests. Here are some of the greatest shopping areas in Durban:

1. Gateway Theatre of Shopping: Located at 1 Palm Boulevard, Umhlanga Ridge, Durban.

Monday through Saturday, 9:00 AM to 9:00 PM; Sunday, 9:00 AM to 6:00 PM.

Gateway Theatre of Shopping, one of the largest shopping malls in the Southern Hemisphere, is Durban's top retail attraction. This enormous mall, located in the bustling Umhlanga Ridge sector, houses over 400 businesses, including top fashion brands, luxury boutiques, and specialist shops. Visitors may enjoy a wide choice of food options, from informal eateries to fine dining restaurants, as well as entertainment activities, including a cinema complex, an indoor climbing wall, and an adventure park. Gateway Theatre of Shopping, with its modern design, energetic ambiance, and vast retail selections, provides a unique shopping and leisure experience for guests of all ages.

2. The Pavilion Shopping Centre is located on Jack Martens Drive in Westville, Durban.

Monday through Saturday, 9:00 AM to 7:00 PM; Sunday, 9:00 AM to 5:00 PM.

The Pavilion Shopping Centre, located in the lush neighborhood of Westville, is a prominent retail hub that serves Durban customers' diversified demands. With over 200 businesses, including major department stores, fashion merchants, and specialized shops, The Pavilion provides a full shopping experience in an accessible location. Visitors may eat at a choice of restaurants and cafés, watch the newest blockbuster at the cinema complex, or participate in family-friendly activities like tenpin bowling and arcade games. The mall's open layout, sufficient parking, and numerous services make it a popular destination for both locals and tourists.

3. Musgrave Centre location: 115 Musgrave Road, Berea, Durban.

Monday through Saturday, 9:00 AM to 7:00 PM; Sunday, 9:00 AM to 5:00 PM.

Musgrave Centre, located in the heart of Durban's Berea area, is a prominent shopping destination recognized for its luxury retailers and exquisite setting. The mall, which has a mix of local and international brands, houses a variety of fashion, beauty, and lifestyle businesses, as well as specialized stores and artisan boutiques. Visitors may unwind and eat at one of the center's several cafés and restaurants or see a movie in the cinema complex. Musgrave Centre's elegant environment and numerous store options give discriminating consumers a premium shopping experience.

4. Durban North Centre is located at 48 Adelaide Tambo Drive in Durban North, Durban.

Monday through Saturday, 9:00 AM to 6:00 PM; Sunday, 9:00 AM to 4:00 PM.

Durban North Centre, situated in the busy area of Durban North, is a popular shopping destination for both locals and visitors. The mall has a wide range of stores, including fashion boutiques, grocers, electronics merchants, and specialized shops, appealing to customers of all ages. Visitors may enjoy a wide range of eating alternatives, including fast food chains and informal cafes, as well as access to critical services like banking and healthcare. Durban North Centre's accessible location, adequate parking, and calm environment make it a great shopping experience for the entire family.

5. Westwood Mall: Located at 16 Lincoln Terrace, Westville, Durban.

Monday through Saturday, 9:00 AM to 7:00 PM; Sunday, 9:00 AM to 5:00 PM.

Westwood Mall, located in the Westville area, is a popular retail center that serves the local population. The mall has a varied selection of stores, including fashion merchants, home décor outlets, electronics stores, and specialized shops, so there's something for everyone. Visitors may eat at the food court or relax in one of the mall's restaurants and cafés. With its accessible location, adequate parking, and family-friendly ambiance, Westwood Mall offers a relaxing shopping experience for people of all ages.

Local Crafts And Souvenirs

Immerse yourself in Durban's unique culture and bring home a piece of its history with these best sites for local crafts and souvenirs. From traditional Zulu beading to modern art pieces, each location provides a one-of-a-kind variety of handcrafted items that capture the essence of Durban. Here's where you can get the greatest local crafts and souvenirs in town:

1. The African Art Centre is located at 94 Florida Road in Windermere, Durban.

Monday through Friday, 9:00 AM to 4:00 PM; Saturday, 9:00 AM to 1:00 PM.

The African Art Centre, located in the fashionable Windermere district, is a long-standing organization that promotes and preserves traditional African art and craftsmanship. The center, which opened in 1959, shows a varied range of handcrafted goods, including finely woven baskets, hand-carved wooden sculptures, vivid fabrics, and beaded jewelry obtained from local craftsmen and cooperatives around South Africa. Visitors may peruse the gallery area and purchase one-of-a-kind souvenirs while helping skilled craftsmen and women earn a living. The African Art Centre, which is committed to ethical commerce and cultural preservation, provides a genuine and stimulating shopping experience for both art enthusiasts and cultural admirers.

2. Victoria Street Market: Located at 151/155 Victoria Street, Durban.

Monday through Saturday, 8:00 AM to 5:00 PM; Sunday, 9:00 AM to 4:00 PM.

The historic Victoria Street Market, located in the heart of Durban's Indian Quarter, transports you to a vibrant world of colors and fragrances. This old market is a treasure trove of African and Indian crafts, with a diverse selection of souvenirs, curios, and mementos to fit every taste or budget. Visitors may browse kiosks filled with homemade things, including beaded jewelry, woven baskets, wooden sculptures, and traditional pottery, as well as scented spices, incense, and textiles. Whether you're searching for a one-of-a-kind present or a souvenir of your trip to Durban, Victoria Street Market offers a lively and colorful shopping experience that highlights the city's ethnic spirit.

3. iHeart Market location: Moses Mabhida Stadium, 44 Isaiah Ntshangase Road, Durban.

Open every first Saturday of the month from 9:00 AM to 2:00 PM.

Experience the ingenuity and craftsmanship of Durban's local craftsmen at the iHeart Market, which takes place monthly at Moses Mabhida Stadium. This colorful market has a carefully chosen range of handcrafted items, such as art, crafts, fashion, and gourmet foods, created by Durban-based independent designers and entrepreneurs. Visitors may peruse stalls selling one-of-a-kind things such as screen-printed fabrics, hand-painted ceramics, upcycled accessories, and organic skincare products, all while enjoying live music and entertainment. iHeart Market provides discriminating consumers with a vibrant and community-focused shopping experience, emphasizing local talent and promoting sustainable consumerism.

4. The Essential Boutique and Gift Shop is located at 100 Florida Road in Windermere, Durban.

Monday through Friday, 8:30 AM to 4:30 PM; Saturday, 9:00 AM to 2:00 PM.

The Essential Boutique & Gift Shop is located in the heart of Durban's dynamic Florida Road area and provides a carefully chosen variety of locally created crafts, artworks, and souvenirs. This quaint store features the work of South African artists and designers, with an emphasis on environmentally friendly and ethically sourced items. Visitors may browse a selection of handcrafted products, such as pottery, textiles, jewelry, and home décor, all of which represent Durban's rich cultural past and creative energy. Whether you're looking for a one-of-a-kind present or a piece of genuine African workmanship, The Essential Boutique and Present Shop offers a lovely shopping experience that highlights local creativity and expertise.

5. Durban Botanic Gardens Gift Shop is located at 9A John Zikhali Road in Berea, Durban.

Monday through Sunday, 8:30 AM to 5:00 PM.

Explore the natural beauty of Durban's oldest botanical gardens and find unique mementos in the Durban Botanic Gardens Gift Shop. This charming store, located inside the gardens' visitor center, sells a carefully chosen variety of souvenirs, books, and botanical-themed products inspired by the garden's rich flora and animals. Visitors may explore a selection of souvenirs, including botanical prints, gardening equipment, herbal teas, and eco-friendly items while admiring the verdant surroundings. Whether you're a nature lover, a plant aficionado, or just searching for a one-of-a-kind souvenir, the Durban Botanic Gardens Gift Shop provides a lovely shopping experience that honors the city's natural history.

DAY TRIPS AND
EXCURSIONS

Durban To Pietermaritzburg

As the sun rises over the beachfront metropolis of Durban, a spirit of adventure pervades. Today, I welcome you to accompany me on an exciting day excursion from Durban to the ancient city of Pietermaritzburg. Buckle up for a voyage through time, culture, and natural beauty.

Our day starts with a lovely drive down the N3 highway, which winds through lush green hills and expansive farmlands. As we leave the metropolitan bustle behind, the calm of the countryside embraces us, providing a quiet escape from the rush and bustle of daily life.

Our first destination on our unforgettable excursion is the legendary Howick Falls, a magnificent cascade that plunges 95 meters into a deep pool below. We step out of the car to be greeted by the waterfall's thunderous roar, its misty spray capturing the early morning light. As we stand in awe of nature's strength, I can't help but think of the rich Zulu legend around these falls, stories about ghosts, and old ceremonies passed down through centuries. After taking in the spectacular splendor of Howick Falls, we continue our journey to Pietermaritzburg, the capital of KwaZulu-Natal province. Pietermaritzburg, renowned for its colonial architecture and bustling cultural scene, provides an intriguing peek into South Africa's eclectic background.

Our first visit to Pietermaritzburg is the ancient City Hall, a beautiful Edwardian structure that dominates the cityscape. As we enter, we are taken back in time to the era of British colonial control as we appreciate the marble staircase and stained glass windows. As we walk through the corridors of this architectural masterpiece, I can't help but wonder at the fine details and artistry that went into its creation.

Next, we visit the Pietermaritzburg Railway Station, a magnificent Victorian-era structure that serves as a reminder of South Africa's railway history. We get onto the station and board the Umgeni Steam Railway, a classic steam train that will take us on a nostalgic ride through the picturesque countryside. As the train chugs down the rails, we travel through lovely scenery interspersed with rolling hills and little settlements. The rhythmic sound of the steam engine relaxes us as we take in the beauty of our surroundings. Our final trip for the day is the Natal Museum, where we will learn about the region's rich history and culture. The museum, which has archeological relics as well as natural history displays, provides an intriguing glimpse into the complex tapestry of life in KwaZulu-Natal.

As the sun sets on our day excursion to Pietermaritzburg, I can't help but be glad for the chance to discover this wonderful city and its surroundings. From magnificent waterfalls to historic sites, our vacation has provided us with memorable memories that will last a lifetime. So, till the next time, Durban, farewell and happy traveling!

Dolphin Coast Tour

The early light pours a golden glow over Durban, our destination for an expedition along the lovely Dolphin Coast. With excitement growing, we head off on our day excursion, anxious to see the treasures that await us along this lovely length of shore.

Our voyage begins with a leisurely drive down the gorgeous coastline road, where the blue seas of the Indian Ocean invite us to discover their mysteries. As we weave our way along the coast, the rhythmic sound of waves breaking against the shore gives a calm soundtrack to our expedition.

Our first destination on the Dolphin Coast is Ballito, a beautiful coastal hamlet famed for its immaculate beaches and relaxed attitude. We step onto the silky, white beaches to be met by joyful dolphins frolicking in the surf, their sleek shapes sliding effortlessly over the waves. With excitement racing through our veins, we join them right away, diving into the crystal-clear waters to swim alongside these gorgeous creatures. Following our thrilling experience with the dolphins, we continued our journey down the coast, pausing at several viewpoint locations to observe the magnificent vistas of the ocean spread out in front of us. With each passing mile, we are enthralled by the beauty of the coastline, its craggy cliffs, and quiet coves that provide unlimited opportunities for exploration and discovery. As the day passes, we are lured to the charming beach community of Salt Rock, where we enjoy a great seafood feast at one of the local eateries. With the salty wind teasing our senses and the flavor of freshly caught fish enticing our taste buds, we enjoy every second of our seaside gastronomic adventure.

The final stop on our Dolphin Coast trip is the famed Thompson's Bay Tidal Pool, a natural rock pool situated among towering cliffs and lush greenery. As we go down the wooden stairway to the water's edge, we are met by the sight of families and friends playing in the cold, clear waters, their laughter combining with the sound of breaking waves.

As the sun begins to set below the horizon, throwing a warm light across the beach, we ponder on the beauty and magic of our Dolphin Coast trip. From spectacular encounters with dolphins to peaceful times by the sea, our tour has been packed with memorable memories that will last long after we return home. And as we say goodbye to this lovely part of the globe, we take with us fond memories of a day spent discovering the Dolphin Coast's beauties.

Valley Of A Thousand Hills

As the sun rises above KwaZulu-Natal's luscious hills, I set off on an incredible excursion through the Valley of a Thousand Hills. With eagerness flowing through my veins, I went out to explore this lovely region, hoping to discover its hidden riches and timeless beauty.

Our adventure begins with a picturesque drive along winding roads that twist through rolling hills and lush valleys. As we go across the countryside, the air becomes filled with the pleasant aroma of wildflowers and the musical chattering of birds, generating a sensation of calm and peace that wraps around us like a loving hug. Our first trip is to the stunning PheZulu Safari Park, where we are met by authentic Zulu houses hidden among lush flora. Stepping out of the car, we are greeted by pleasant folks dressed in vivid traditional clothing, ready to share their rich cultural history with us.

As we wander through the park, we are treated to a captivating show of Zulu dance and music, with the rhythmic beat of the drums and the elegant movements of the dancers taking us to another time and place. With each step, we immerse ourselves in Zulu culture's brilliant colors and rhythms, deepening our respect for the traditions and practices passed down through centuries. After our cultural experience, we continue our trek deeper into the valley, where we come upon the breathtaking Inanda Dam. The dam, which stretches out before us like a dazzling blue oasis, provides a peaceful getaway from the rush and bustle of daily life. With its peaceful waters and panoramic views of the surrounding hills, it is the ideal place to rest and unwind while taking in nature's splendor.

As the day comes to a close, we make our way to the well-known Shongweni Farmers Market, where we are welcomed by the inviting scent of freshly baked bread and roasted coffee. Amidst the busy booths and energetic conversation of merchants and guests alike, we enjoy a sensory feast, enjoying wonderful local dishes and artisan handicrafts.

As I ponder on the day's events, I am overwhelmed with deep appreciation for having the chance to visit the Valley of a Thousand Hills. From its breathtaking natural scenery to its rich cultural legacy, this enchanted location has left an unforgettable imprint on my heart, reminding me of the beauty and wonder that surrounds us daily. And as I say goodbye to this magnificent part of the globe, I bring with me fond recollections of a day spent discovering the Valley of a Thousand Hills' hidden treasures.

EVENTS AND FESTIVALS

Durban July

Every year, the city of Durban comes alive with an exciting atmosphere as both locals and visitors congregate to celebrate one of the most renowned events on the South African social calendar: Durban July. This legendary horse racing event, held at Greyville Racecourse, is a sight of glamor, fashion, and exciting horse racing action that draws thousands of fans from all over the country.

Durban July has a strong history dating back to 1897, making it a popular festival. Originally intended to highlight the region's best-thoroughbred horses, the event has grown into a glitzy spectacle that combines high-stakes racing, high dress, and entertainment. Over the years, Durban July has been synonymous with elegance, flair, and status, attracting a varied throng of race fans, fashionistas, and socialites. Durban July is a fashion extravaganza when guests dress to impress in their finest apparel. From bold statement hats to spectacular couture dresses, the event celebrates sartorial grandeur and inventiveness. Each year, a theme is chosen, allowing visitors to interpret it in their own distinct manner, culminating in a stunning display of fashion-forward ensembles that equal the thrill of the horse races themselves. Fashion contests and best-dressed awards add to the glitz, making Durban July a haven for fashion enthusiasts and trendsetters. Durban July is known for its world-class horse racing activities rather than just fashion. The event includes a number of high-profile events, including the coveted Durban July Handicap, which draws some of the best horses, trainers, and jockeys from throughout the country. From the thundering hooves of the sprint races to the nail-biting finishes of the major event, the track is alive with excitement, keeping fans on the tip of their seats throughout the day.

Durban July provides a variety of entertainment and hospitality opportunities to complement the exciting racing and spectacular attire. There are several ways to experience the event in grandeur, including VIP marquees and hospitality suites that provide gourmet cuisine and premium beverages, as well as live music performances and celebrity guests. Whether you're drinking champagne on the track or dancing the night away at one of the VIP after-parties, Durban July ensures a unique experience for everyone who attends. Durban July is not only a major horse racing event but also a cultural phenomenon that unites individuals from many backgrounds together. It is a celebration of South African culture, diversity, and togetherness, bringing people from all backgrounds together to share in the atmosphere of camaraderie and enthusiasm. From the roar of the fans as the horses race down the track to the triumphant cries as the victors cross the finish line, Durban July embodies South Africa's lively and energetic character.

To summarize, Durban July is more than simply a horse racing event; it is a festival of flair, refinement, and excitement that captures the spirit of Durban's diverse culture and tradition. With its combination of world-class racing, high fashion, and entertainment, Durban July provides an unparalleled event that continues to fascinate and inspire all attendees.

Cultural Festivals

Visit one of Durban's lively and dynamic cultural events to immerse yourself in the city's rich tapestry of cultural history. These events provide a riveting view into the different cultures that make Durban home, featuring traditional music and dance as well as celebrating local cuisine and crafts. Discover the enchantment of these cultural events by exploring the sights, sounds, and flavors that characterize Durban's cultural scene.

1. Essence Festival Durban celebrates African culture and creativity, making it a cultural landmark for the city. This exciting event brings together singers, artists, entrepreneurs, and thought leaders from all over the continent to honor African greatness and innovation. From thrilling concerts by prominent African singers to thought-provoking debates about business and entrepreneurship, Essence Festival Durban provides a forum for inspiration, empowerment, and celebration.

2. Durban International Film Festival: One of Africa's longest-running film festivals, it exhibits a broad variety of local and international films reflecting the region's rich cultural diversity. From thought-provoking documentaries to cutting-edge feature films, this famous festival draws filmmakers, industry experts, and cinema aficionados from all over the world. The Durban International Film Festival, with its screenings, seminars, and panel discussions, provides a unique chance to connect with cinematic narrative while also celebrating the art of filmmaking.

3. Durban Fashion Fair: This yearly event showcases local talent and originality, offering a glimpse into the

glamorous world of fashion. Featuring runway displays, pop-up stores, and fashion seminars, this event highlights Durban's dynamic fashion culture while also providing a platform for young designers to showcase their designs. The Durban Fashion Fair celebrates South African fashion's diversity and inventiveness, featuring avant-garde designs as well as traditional clothes with a modern touch.

4. Durban International Blues Festival: Experience the deep sounds of the blues. This yearly event brings together blues musicians from all around the world for a weekend of thrilling shows, jam sessions, and workshops. Whether you're a die-hard blues fan or just like fine music, the Durban International Blues Festival provides an amazing experience full of passion, rhythm, and soul.

5. Durban Diwali Festival: Celebrate the festival of lights with the colorful Durban Diwali Festival, which brings together the city's Indian community to celebrate the triumph of light over darkness. From spectacular fireworks displays to traditional music and dance performances, this festive celebration is a sensory feast for people of all ages. Sample excellent Indian cuisine, buy festive clothes and decorations and soak up the festive mood of Durban's Diwali celebrations.

6. Durban Jazz Festival: This yearly event celebrates the soul-stirring melodies and seductive rhythms of jazz music. This festival, which includes performances by local and worldwide jazz performers, seminars, masterclasses, and jam sessions, celebrates jazz music's diversity and originality. Whether you're a seasoned jazz fan or simply like fine music, the Durban Jazz Festival

provides an exciting experience that will have you tapping Your Feet And Humming Along With The Beat.

Food And Wine Events

Enjoy the aromas of Durban's dynamic culinary scene with a tour of its tempting food and wine events. From gourmet feasts to wine tastings and culinary courses, these events provide a delicious opportunity to sample the city's numerous gastronomic offers. Take a culinary journey as you discover the rich flavors, smells, and textures that distinguish Durban's food and wine culture.

1. Durban Food and Wine Festival: This yearly event highlights the city's vibrant food and wine sector. This event, which features a delicious selection of gourmet foods, exquisite wines, and artisanal items, highlights the finest of Durban's culinary offerings. The Durban Food and Wine Festival promises a feast for the senses, with celebrity chef demos, wine-matching sessions, and gastronomic seminars to leave you wanting more.

2. Durban Street Food Festival: Enjoy the colorful flavors and fragrances of Durban's street food scene. This bustling event brings together food trucks, merchants, and chefs from all across the city to display their trademark dishes and inventive culinary creations. The Durban Street Food Festival features a wide variety of street foods that reflect the city's ethnic past, from fiery bunny chows to juicy shisanyama and delectable samoosas. With live music, entertainment, and gastronomic competitions, this event is a must-see for anybody who enjoys wonderful cuisine and colorful street culture.

3. Durban Wine and Dine Festival: Celebrate Durban's growing wine culture with a sophisticated event that combines wine tasting and gourmet eating. Set against the background of the city's picturesque surroundings, this

festival encourages wine lovers to try a diverse range of local and international wines combined with wonderful foods made by renowned chefs and restaurants. From crisp whites to full-bodied reds, the Durban Wine and Dine Festival takes you on a sensory voyage across the wine world, complete with live music, wine education seminars, and culinary displays.

4. Durban Craft Beer and Food Festival: For beer lovers and foodies alike! The Durban Craft Beer and Food Festival celebrates craft brewing and gourmet cuisine by displaying Durban's greatest local beers and culinary delicacies. Sample a variety of handmade beers from the city's microbreweries combined with artisanal cheeses, charcuterie, and other tasty delights. This festival, which includes live music, beer-making workshops, and beer-matching sessions, provides a unique chance to explore the flavors and smells of Durban's expanding craft beer sector.

5. Durban Seafood and Wine Festival celebrates the city's abundant seafood choices. From luscious prawns and juicy oysters to grilled fish and seafood paella, this festival serves up a delectable selection of ocean-inspired cuisine matched with superb wines from the region. The Durban Seafood and Wine Festival, which includes top chef culinary demos, seafood sampling, and wine-matching seminars, is a must-see event for both seafood and wine fans.

LANGUAGE AND CULTURE

Zulu Language Basics

As you embark on your journey to explore the vibrant culture of KwaZulu-Natal, immerse yourself in the rich tapestry of the Zulu language. With its melodious tones and expressive phrases, Zulu is a language that reflects the warmth and hospitality of its people. Whether you're greeting locals, ordering food, or simply engaging in conversation, learning a few basic phrases in Zulu will enhance your travel experience and foster meaningful connections with the local community. Here are some essential Zulu language basics to help you navigate your way through your adventures:

1. Greetings:

Sawubona (sah-woo-BOH-nah) - Hello (when addressing one person)

Sanibonani (sah-nee-boh-NAH-nee) - Hello (when addressing multiple people)

Unjani? (oon-JAH-nee) - How are you? (singular)

Ninjani? (nee-JAH-nee) - How are you? (plural)

2. Common Phrases:

Ngiyabonga (nee-yah-BONG-gah) - Thank you

Yebo (YEH-boh) - Yes

Cha (CHAH) - No

Ukudla (oo-KOO-dlah) - Food

Iphi indawo yomculo? (ee-pee een-DAH-woh yoh-moo-CLOH) - Where is the music venue?

3. Numbers:

Kunye (koo-NYEH) - One

Kubili (koo-BEE-lee) - Two

Kuthathu (koo-TAH-too) - Three

Kune (koo-NEH) - Four

Kuyisithupha (koo-yee-SEE-too-pah) - Five

4. Basic Conversational Phrases:

Ngicela amanzi (ngi-SEH-lah ah-MAN-zee) - Please bring water

Ngicela ukufunda (ngi-SEH-lah oo-koo-FOON-dah) - Please teach me

Ungathanda ukudlela nami? (oon-gah-TAHN-dah oo-koo-DLAY-lah NAH-mee) - Would you like to eat with me?

Ngiphendule kahle (ngi-PHEN-doo-leh kah-KLEH) - Please speak slowly

5. Expressions of Appreciation:

Hamba kahle (HAM-bah kah-KLEH) - Go well (Goodbye)

Sala kahle (SAH-lah kah-KLEH) - Stay well (Goodbye)

Ngiyavuma (nee-yah-VOO-mah) - I agree

Ngiyaxolisa (nee-yah-sho-LEE-sah) - I apologize

By familiarizing yourself with these basic Zulu language phrases, you'll not only enhance your travel experience but also show respect for the local culture and traditions. So, embrace the beauty of Zulu language and let it enrich your journey through the heartland of South Africa. Sawubona!

Cultural Etiquette

Understanding and respecting local traditions and etiquette is vital for a meaningful and engaging experience while immersed in Durban's unique cultural scene. From greetings to dining traditions, here's a complete guide to cultural etiquette in Durban.

1. Hello:

When meeting someone for the first time, a handshake is a customary greeting in Durban. However, among friends and family, it is usual to welcome with a warm embrace or a cheek kiss.

When addressing seniors or individuals in positions of power, it is appropriate to use titles such as "Mr.," "Mrs.," "Auntie", and "Uncle" followed by their surname.

In Zulu culture, it is usual to welcome with "Sawubona" (pronounced sah-woo-boh-nah), which means "I see you," and to respond with "Yebo" (pronounced yeh-boh), which means "Yes, I see you."

2. Respect for the Elders:

Respect for elders is firmly embedded in Zulu culture. When engaging with seniors, it is traditional to express respect and humility through language and gestures.

When seated in a gathering, it is customary to allow seniors to sit first and to serve them food or drinks before serving oneself.

3. Dinner Etiquette:

When invited to someone's house for supper, it is courteous to attend on time or somewhat early.

It is usual to wait for the host to start the dinner before eating. Once the dinner has begun, it is customary to wait for the eldest or most senior member to start eating before you begin.

When dining with your hands, as is customary in Zulu culture, only use your right hand to eat, as the left hand is considered filthy.

4. Dress Code:

While Durban is a cosmopolitan city with a variety of fashion trends, it is vital to dress modestly, particularly while visiting religious sites or attending cultural activities.

When visiting rural regions or traditional Zulu villages, dress conservatively to honor local customs and traditions.

5. Language, Communication:

While English is frequently spoken in Durban, knowing a few simple Zulu words may go a long way toward demonstrating respect for the local culture and encouraging constructive relationships.

Avoid using slang or casual language, especially when speaking with seniors or people in positions of power.

6. Sacred Sites and Traditions.

When visiting holy locations or engaging in traditional ceremonies, it is critical to honor and respect the local community's customs and beliefs.

Before taking pictures or participating in any rites or ceremonies, seek permission from local guides or community leaders, and always follow their instructions.

By adopting and sticking to these cultural etiquette norms, you will not only demonstrate respect for Durban's rich traditions but will also strengthen your relationship with the local community and create important and unforgettable experiences throughout your stay.

Traditional Customs

Durban, a melting pot of cultures, has a rich tapestry of traditional practices that represent the variety and background of its inhabitants. From ancient ceremonies to modern-day festivals, here's a complete introduction to Durban's traditional customs:

1. Zulu Ceremony:

The Zulus, one of South Africa's major ethnic groupings, have maintained numerous ancient rituals and ceremonies.

The "Umemulo," or coming-of-age event, commemorates a young woman's entrance into womanhood. During Umemulo, the young woman wears traditional clothes and participates in ceremonies that symbolize her readiness for marriage.

Another significant Zulu festival is the "Umhlanga," or Reed Dance, in which unmarried Zulu females assemble to honor their chastity and purity. The highlight of the ritual is a dance done by thousands of young ladies dressed in colorful outfits and holding reeds to gift to the Zulu monarch.

2. Traditional dress:

Traditional Zulu dress is an important part of cultural festivals and events. Men frequently wear "isibheshu," a skirt made of animal skin, along with a beaded belt and headgear.

Women typically wear "isidwaba," a wraparound skirt, with an "ithayi," a beaded bodice, and beaded jewelry such as necklaces, bracelets, and anklets.

116

Beadwork is an essential component of Zulu culture, with each color and pattern carrying symbolic meaning and value.

3. Sangoma and Traditional Healing.

Sangomas, or traditional healers, have an important role in Zulu culture, acting as bridges between the physical and spiritual realms.

Sangomas go through rigorous training and initiation procedures to learn about ancient medicinal methods, herbal cures, and spiritual advice.

Consultations with sangomas frequently include rituals like divination with bones or other artifacts to diagnose ailments and provide direction and treatment.

4. Traditional Music and Dance.

Zulu culture is built around music and dance, with rhythmic drumming and vigorous dances demonstrating the community's energy and enthusiasm.

Traditional Zulu dances, such as the "Indlamu" (Zulu war dance) and "Ukukhamba" (heel-toe dance), are performed at various festivities and gatherings while singing and ululating.

The dances are accompanied by rhythmic rhythms and melodies created by instruments such as the "umakhweyana" (traditional bow) and the "izintonga" (knobkerrie).

5. Cultural Celebrations and Festivals:

Durban celebrates a variety of cultural festivities and festivals throughout the year, giving visitors the opportunity to experience local practices firsthand.

The Durban Cultural Festival, Zulu Past Day, and Umhlanga Festival all display traditional music, dance, arts, crafts, and food, providing tourists with a look into Durban's rich cultural past.

These festivals provide opportunities to preserve and promote cultural practices while also instilling a feeling of communal pride and solidarity.

6. Respect for the Elders and Ancestors:

Respect for elders and ancestors is firmly established in Zulu culture, with rites and ceremonies commemorating those who have passed away.

Ancestral worship, also known as "amadlozi," entails rituals and gifts to placate and seek advice from ancestral spirits, who are thought to play an important part in the lives of humans.

Elders are respected for their knowledge and experience, and their advice is sought on issues of family, community, and tradition.

By discovering and embracing these ancient rituals, visitors to Durban can develop a better knowledge and respect for the city's rich cultural legacy. From formal rites to lively festivities, Durban's ancient customs reveal the heart and spirit of its people.

HEALTH AND WELLNESS

Spa Retreats

Escape the hustle and bustle of daily life and go on a journey of relaxation and renewal at the magnificent spa resorts located in the heart of Durban. From serene surroundings to sumptuous treatments, each spa provides a haven for you to relax, replenish, and restore your mind, body, and soul. Here's all you need to know about spa getaways in Durban:

1. Location and Ambience:

Durban offers a wide range of spa getaways, from quiet coastal resorts to tranquil hideaways set among lush foliage.

Each spa is deliberately constructed to offer a quiet and appealing environment, complete with soothing music, fragrant smells, and tranquil settings that transport you to a state of blissful relaxation.

2. Spa treatments:

Spa getaways in Durban provide a diverse range of services to meet your every desire, from sumptuous massages to reviving facials and energizing body scrubs.

Whether you want a classic Swedish massage to relax tired muscles or a lavish aromatherapy session to quiet your mind, professional therapists can tailor each experience to your needs.

3. Signature experiences:

Many spa getaways in Durban provide trademark experiences that highlight the region's natural beauty and cultural history. These experiences provide a genuinely immersive spa visit, with indigenous botanical treatments utilizing locally obtained materials as well as traditional African healing rites.

Indulge in a trademark African-inspired treatment, such as a Marula oil massage or a Rooibos-infused facial, which are intended to nourish the skin and stimulate the senses.

4. Wellness facilities:

In addition to spa treatments, many retreats provide wellness amenities such as steam rooms, saunas, and hydrotherapy pools, where you may relax and purify your body.

Take a plunge in a heated pool with a view of the beach, or relax in a peaceful garden refuge surrounded by rich tropical flora and the calming sound of trickling waterfalls.

5. Holistic Healing Practices.

Some spa vacations in Durban provide holistic therapeutic activities like yoga, meditation, and mindfulness seminars to improve overall well-being and inner harmony.

Immerse yourself in a guided meditation session on the beach at sunrise, or attend a yoga class in a tranquil garden setting to reconnect with yourself and achieve inner peace.

6. Personalized wellness programs:

121

Many spa resorts provide individualized wellness programs that are geared to your specific requirements and goals.

Whether you want to detoxify and cleanse, renew and revitalize, or just rest and unwind, skilled practitioners are here to help you on your path to maximum health.

From the minute you enter a Durban spa retreat, you will be engulfed in a sense of calm and peace that will restore your body, soothe your mind, and feed your spirit. Whether you're looking for a relaxing holiday or a transforming health experience, Durban's spa retreats provide a safe haven where you can reconnect with yourself and emerge feeling cleansed, revived, and invigorated.

Yoga Studios

Embark on a voyage of self-discovery and total well-being at the tranquil yoga studios sprinkled across Durban. These studios provide a retreat from the strains of contemporary life, allowing you to reconnect with your body, mind, and soul through the practice of yoga. Here's what you should know about yoga studios in Durban:

1. Various Styles:

Durban's yoga studios provide a wide selection of yoga styles to accommodate practitioners of all skill levels and interests. Everyone may find something to like, from vigorous vinyasa flow to gentle hatha yoga, soothing yin yoga, and strong ashtanga yoga.

You'll find a class that suits your requirements, whether you want a hard exercise to increase strength and flexibility or a relaxing practice to calm the mind and release stress.

2. Experienced Instructors:

Each yoga studio in Durban is staffed by skilled and qualified yoga instructors who are eager to share the transforming effects of yoga with their students.

Whether you're a novice or a seasoned practitioner, teachers are committed to offering customized coaching, alignment cues, and changes to guarantee a safe and satisfying experience.

3. A welcoming atmosphere:

When you go into any yoga class in Durban, you'll be met with a warm and friendly environment that encourages you to leave your troubles at the door and immerse yourself in the present now.

Each studio is intended to provide a sense of peace and serenity that enhances your yoga experience, with soft lighting and peaceful decor, as well as the soothing sounds of nature and quiet music.

4. Community Connections:

Yoga studios in Durban serve as dynamic community hubs where like-minded people may support and encourage one another on their yoga journeys.

Whether you're attending a group class, taking part in a workshop or retreat, or simply having a cup of tea and discussion after class, you'll feel a feeling of community and connection that will enhance your yoga practice.

5. Specialized offerings:

In addition to conventional yoga courses, many Durban studios provide specialty services like pregnant yoga, children's yoga, yoga therapy, meditation classes, and workshops on themes ranging from mindfulness to Ayurveda.

These specialist options offer opportunities for further research and advancement, allowing you to personalize your practice to your individual requirements and interests.

6. Holistic Wellness Service:

Some yoga studios in Durban include holistic wellness services like massage treatment, acupuncture, energy healing, and nutritional counseling to supplement your yoga practice and improve your overall health.

These integrated wellness practices offer a comprehensive foundation for health and healing, allowing you to create balance, energy, and resilience in your body, mind, and spirit.

Whether you're an experienced yogi or new to the discipline, Durban's yoga studios provide a safe haven where you may nurture your body, relax your mind, and raise your soul. Yoga's transforming power can help you find a greater feeling of connection, balance, and vigor, enriching all parts of your life.

PHOTOGRAPHY GUIDE

Best Photography Spots

Discover Durban's stunning splendor via your lens as you explore its different landscapes, prominent monuments, and hidden jewels. From breathtaking beaches to vivid street art, Durban provides a plethora of picture options for both amateur and professional photographers. Here's a list of the greatest photography places in Durban:

1. The Umhlanga Rocks Lighthouse:

The Umhlanga Rocks Lighthouse, perched on a rocky outcrop overlooking the Indian Ocean, is a well-known landmark of Durban's coastline. Capture beautiful views of the lighthouse against a backdrop of crashing waves and golden sunsets, resulting in amazing photographs that highlight the region's natural beauty.

2. Durban Botanical Gardens:

Discover the quiet sanctuary of the Durban Botanic Gardens, which has lush foliage, vivid flowers, and picturesque strolling routes. Photograph the stunning landscapes, vibrant blossoms, and tranquil water features to capture the spirit of nature's beauty in the middle of the city.

3. Moses Mabhida Stadium:

Moses Mabhida Stadium, an architectural masterpiece and icon of contemporary Durban, provides photographers with unique viewpoints and angles.

Capture breathtaking shots of the stadium's distinctive arch, sweeping curves, and urban environs, contrasting modern architecture with the metropolitan skyline.

4. Street Art at Station Drive Precinct

Wander around the vivid streets of the Station Drive Precinct, where colorful murals and street art decorate the walls, providing an exciting setting for photography. Document the diverse range of urban art, capturing the ingenuity and expression of local artists against the backdrop of industrial architecture.

5. Golden Mile Beach:

The Golden Mile Beachfront, which stretches along Durban's coastline, provides an abundance of opportunity to capture the spirit of coastal living. Photograph surfers surfing the waves, sunbathers bathing in the sun, and families having picnics on the sandy shoreline to capture the relaxed atmosphere and natural beauty of Durban's beach culture.

6. Victoria St. Market:

Immerse yourself in the bright ambiance of Victoria Street Market, where busy kiosks are filled with colorful spices, fabrics, and handicrafts. Capture the rush and bustle of market life by shooting the brilliant colors, intricate patterns, and various faces that reflect Durban's global past.

7. Ugeni River Bird Park:

Enter a world of natural beauty and avian delights at the Umgeni River Bird Park, which is home to a wide array of exotic birds from all over the world.

Photograph beautiful birds in flight, intimate moments of feeding and nesting, and relax in the tranquil settings of lush flora and tumbling waterfalls.

8. Kwa Muhle Museum:

The KwaMuhle Museum, located in a historic structure that originally housed the city's Native Administration Department, offers a glimpse into Durban's rich history and legacy. Document the museum's exhibits, architectural features, and emotive items to tell the story of Durban's past and people's perseverance.

9. Valley of the Thousand Hills:

Explore the Valley of a Thousand Hills magnificent sceneries, which feature undulating hills, flowing rivers, and traditional Zulu homesteads. Photograph spectacular landscapes from beautiful locations, document true rural life, and immerse yourself in South Africa's timeless beauty.

10. Durban harbor:

Explore the bustling action of Durban Harbour, one of Africa's largest ports, where enormous cargo ships, fishing boats, and waterfront monuments provide plenty of picture opportunities. Capture the harbor's vibrant vitality by capturing the colorful boats, bustling marketplaces, and sweeping views of the waterfront skyline against the backdrop of the Indian Ocean.

From sweeping coastline vistas to colorful urban settings, Durban's photographic places provide a plethora of opportunities to capture the soul of this dynamic city. Whether you're a seasoned photographer or a beginner, let your imagination run wild as you discover the different landscapes and cultural riches that lie around every turn.

Tips For Capturing Durban's Essence

With these professional suggestions, you'll learn how to capture Durban's dynamic personality and natural beauty via your lens. Whether you're a seasoned photographer or a novice enthusiast, these tips can help you create great photographs that capture the soul of this vibrant city.

1. Embrace Light:

Durban is blessed with plenty of sunshine, making it great for outdoor photography. Use gentle morning light or the golden hues of sunset to give warmth and depth to your photographs. Experiment with various lighting settings to get dramatic effects, such as catching the shimmering reflections of city lights on water or the gentle glow of dawn emerging over the horizon.

2. Investigate Different Perspectives:

Don't be afraid to step off the main path and discover lesser-known communities and hidden gems. From vibrant street markets to historic sites, Durban has a plethora of picture options waiting to be explored. Look for new angles and views that highlight Durban's variety, whether you're photographing the city skyline from a rooftop or street scenes from the ground.

3. Capture the Cultural Tapestry.

Durban is a cultural melting pot, and its dynamic cultural environment inspires photographers on a continuous basis. Capture the vivid clothes and expressive movements of Zulu dancers at a traditional celebration, as well as the precise features of Hindu temples decked up in vibrant decorations.

Engage with local communities and immerse yourself in their habits and traditions to capture genuine moments that showcase Durban's diverse cultural history.

4. Concentrate on landscapes and seascapes:

Durban is a nature photographer's dream, with its breathtaking coastline, abundant flora, and picturesque scenery. Explore the craggy cliffs and sandy beaches of the coast, visit lush nature reserves, or go inland to the Valley of a Thousand Hills. Experiment with different compositions and focus points to capture the natural beauty of Durban's landscapes, such as the sweeping curves of a beach, the vivid colors of a sunset, or the serene serenity of a waterfall.

5. Tell a Story Through Your Photos:

Beyond shooting stunning shots, try to communicate a story through your photographs. Whether you're recording Durban inhabitants' everyday lives, capturing the energy of a crowded market, or exhibiting the city's architectural treasures, let your images elicit emotions and pique interest. Look for moments of spontaneity and authenticity that capture the essence of Durban's colorful culture and dynamic energy, such as a frank grin, a fleeting look, or a moment of calm reflection.

6. Be prepared and patient.

Photography is all about being in the right location at the right moment. Keep your camera equipment clean, charged, and ready to use at any time. Be patient and watchful, letting situations emerge organically and capturing them with accuracy and delicacy. Remember

131

that the finest images usually appear when you least expect them.

Following these ideas and methods will prepare you to capture the essence of Durban and create magnificent photographs that showcase the city's colorful culture, breathtaking scenery, and dynamic personality. So grab your camera, keep an open mind, and let your imagination fly as you take a photography tour around Durban's various beautiful landscapes.

PLANNING YOUR TRIP

Itinerary Suggestions

Day 1: Cultural immersion.

Morning: Begin your adventure by visiting the KwaMuhle Museum, where you'll learn about Durban's rich history and cultural legacy.

Afternoon: Visit the lively Victoria Street Market and sample local specialties such as rabbit chow and samosas.

Evening: Have dinner at a traditional South African restaurant and experience the flavors of local food.

Day Two: Coastal Exploration

Morning: Spend the day visiting Durban's beachfront, soaking up the sun, and participating in water activities like surfing and paddleboarding.

Afternoon: Visit the landmark Umhlanga Rocks Lighthouse and walk along the picturesque promenade.

Evening: Dine at a beachside restaurant while watching the sunset over the Indian Ocean.

Day 3: Nature & Wildlife

Morning: Explore the beautiful landscapes of Durban Botanic Gardens, marveling at the various flora and wildlife.

Afternoon: Visit Umgeni River Bird Park for up-close encounters with unique species from throughout the world.

Evening: Relax at your lodgings or explore Durban's thriving nightlife scene.

Day Four: Adventure and Thrills

Morning: Ride the SkyCar at Moses Mabhida Stadium for a panoramic view of the city.

Afternoon: Spend the day at uShaka Marine World, where you may snorkel, scuba dive, and go shark cage diving.

Evening: Dine at one of the restaurants on uShaka Village Walk while enjoying live music and entertainment.

Day Five: Cultural Heritage

Morning: Explore the Station Drive Precinct, with its vivid street art and unique businesses.

Afternoon: Visit the Phansi Museum to learn about Zulu culture and heritage.

Evening: Attend a traditional Zulu cultural show and feast.

Day Six: Relaxation and Wellness.

Morning: Begin your day with a yoga class at a local facility that overlooks the beach.

Afternoon: Spend the day relaxing at one of Durban's luxury spa resorts, where you may enjoy massages, facials, and other treatments.

Evening: Take a relaxing sunset cruise around Durban's beachfront, seeing the city skyline from the ocean.

Day 7: Outdoor Adventure.

Morning: Hike or mountain bike through the Valley of a Thousand Hills, discovering stunning scenery and traditional Zulu settlements.

Afternoon: Enjoy a picnic lunch overlooking the valley before returning to Durban.

Evening: On your final night in Durban, have a goodbye supper at a rooftop restaurant, toasting memorable memories formed throughout your visit.

Experience the best of Durban's culture, wildlife, and adventure with this thorough 7-day itinerary, which is designed to highlight the city's numerous attractions and give a memorable experience for all visitors.

Packing Tips

Preparing for your trip to Durban necessitates careful planning on what to bring to guarantee a comfortable and happy visit. Here are some important packing recommendations to help you make the most of your visit to this dynamic city.

1. Pack lightweight, breathable clothing made of natural fibers such as cotton or linen for the warm and humid atmosphere of Durban. Choose loose-fitting clothing to keep cool and comfortable during your adventures.

2. Sun Protection: When there's a lot of sun, it's important to bring sunscreen. Bring a wide-brimmed hat, UV-protective sunglasses, and a high-SPF sunscreen to protect your skin from the sun's rays, especially if you expect to spend time outside.

3. Pack your swimsuit and beach supplies to explore Durban's stunning beaches. Whether you're swimming, sunbathing, or engaging in water sports, having the proper equipment can help you make the most of your time at the beach.

4. Insect Repellent: When visiting Durban's natural attractions or dining outside, use insect repellent to avoid mosquitoes and other pests. Bring a DEET-based repellent to protect yourself from pest bites, especially during the warmer months.

5. Bring appropriate walking shoes or sandals to explore Durban's many attractions, including busy downtown streets and stunning mountain paths. Choose footwear with appropriate support and traction to keep your feet comfortable throughout the day.

137

6. Light Rain Gear: Durban receives periodic rains, especially during summer. Pack a small rain jacket or umbrella to keep you dry in the event of an unexpected rain shower, allowing you to continue exploring uninterrupted.

7. Pack a universal travel adaptor to charge electrical gadgets and keep them connected while traveling. Don't forget to pack chargers for your phone, camera, and other electronic devices to record and film your Durban journey.

8. Pack vital prescriptions and a basic first-aid kit, including adhesive bandages, disinfectant wipes, and pain relievers. It is best to be prepared for small situations while traveling.

9. Bring a reusable water bottle to stay hydrated on your Durban journey. Fill it up with filtered water from your hotel or public water fountains to keep hydrated while reducing plastic waste.

10. Travel Documents and Essentials: Pack your passport, visa (if applicable), travel insurance details, and any reservation confirmations. Keep these goods organized and readily available during your vacation.

Follow this packing advice, and you'll be ready to enjoy all Durban has to offer, from its beautiful beaches and cultural attractions to its active nightlife and outdoor activities. Remember to travel light, be comfortable, and embrace the spirit of adventure as you explore this vibrant city.

CONCLUSION

As we near the end of our tour through the lively city of Durban, we can't help but be filled with amazement and wonder at the experiences and memories we've shared. From the golden beaches and verdant landscapes to the rich cultural tapestry and vibrant metropolitan environment, Durban has caught our hearts and awakened our senses in ways we never expected. Throughout this book, we've looked at the various attractions and hidden jewels that make Durban a really unique destination. We've immersed ourselves in the city's rich history and cultural legacy, enjoyed its gastronomic pleasures, and explored its natural beauties. We've laughed, learned, and fallen in love with every part of this magical city.

But our adventure does not stop here. As you conclude this book, I urge you to embark on your own journey to Durban and experience its charm firsthand. Durban has something for everyone, whether you want to relax on gorgeous beaches, go on thrilling excursions, or explore the city's rich culture. So what are you waiting for? Pack your luggage, buy your flights, and be ready to be carried away by Durban's beauty and intrigue. Whether you're a seasoned traveler or going on your first journey, Durban guarantees to exceed your expectations and leave you with life-long memories.

Join us as we say goodbye to this wonderful city, knowing that while our adventure ends here, the spirit of Durban will continue to inspire and enchant us long after we leave. Take the chance and discover Durban for yourself. Your journey awaits.

Made in the USA
Columbia, SC
24 October 2024

44988950R00078